CALLING THE MIDWEST HOME

Calling the Midwest Home

*A Lively Look at the Origins, Attitudes, Quirks, and
Curiosities of America's Heartlanders*

CAROLYN LIEBERG

Foreword by Bob Greene

WILDCAT CANYON PRESS
A Division of Circulus Publishing Group, Inc.
Berkeley, California

Publisher: Julienne Bennett
Editors: Julienne Bennett and Roy M. Carlisle
Copyeditor: Deborah Miller
Cover Design: Big Fish
Interior Design & Page Layout: Gordon Chun Design

Wildcat Canyon Press
2716 Ninth Street
Berkeley, CA 94710
Phone (510) 848-3600
Fax   (510) 848-1326
Email Circulus@aol.com

LIBRARY OF CONGRESS CATALOGING-IN-PUBLICATION DATA

Lieberg, Carolyn S.
    Calling the Midwest home: a lively look at the origins, attitudes, quirks, and curiosities of America's heartlanders / Carolyn Lieberg.
    p. cm.
ISBN 1-885171-12-9 (pbk.)
    1. Middle West—Social life and customs—Miscellanea. 2. Middle West—History, Local—Miscellanea. 3. Middle West—Biography—Miscellanea. I. Title.
F351.L54 1996
978—dc20   96-32107
                                                                      CIP

Printed in the United States of America
Distributed to the trade by Publishers Group West
10 9 8 7 6 5 4 3 2 1

CONTENTS

ACKNOWLEDGMENTS

My thanks to Julie Bennett, whose midwestern roots inspired the vision for this book and whose love and faith in the Midwest guided me; Roy M. Carlisle for his professionalism, his forbearance, and his willingness to try to understand whatever this midwestern *shtick* is; to Tamara Traeder, Holly A. Taines, and Rose Bargmann for assistance and support; to Gordon and Suzanne Chun for their design wizardry, hard work, and for caring. And the "Mags" for doing what loyal dogs do.

A large thank you to the many people who helped me gather information—some of you wrote books or articles I consulted, some of you answered my telephone calls for clarification of this or that, and you were all, of course, polite and helpful. My parents, Ad and Odd, and my daughters, Adria and Rachel, my brother and his family, Jerry, Dee, Lauren, and Shannon, and my wonderful in-laws all supplied cheery support, and some of you gave me terrific ideas.

Specific nominees for "most helpful in the face of deadlines and difficult questions" are numerous librarians in Iowa City, researcher Daryl Brand, my stepson Given Johnson, and library friends at the Carnegie Foundation for the Advancement of Teaching. The Oscar, however, for his tireless and unwavering good cheer during this process goes—with no bias whatsoever—to my husband the saint, Craig Johnson, who knows the library catalog system by heart and not only helped me find what I needed to find, but tolerated my involvement in this project with unconditional patience and love. Boy, am I ever lucky.

Thank you, everyone.

DEDICATION

To all Midwesterners everywhere,
especially to my oh-so-midwestern family—
my parents, Addie and Odd Lieberg (as midwestern as you can get)
and my children, Adria and Rachel Hardesty, Given Johnson,
and my husband, Craig Johnson.

And to those who live in:

Illinois

Indiana

Iowa

Kansas

Michigan

Minnesota

Missouri

Nebraska

North Dakota

Ohio

South Dakota

Wisconsin

FOREWORD

There is a phrase that is often used by people who live in New York, Washington, D.C., and Los Angeles to describe those of us who live in the Midwest: "fly-over people."

It means what it sounds like. We are the people whom the so-called power elite on both coasts fly over on their way back and forth to meet with one another about matters of business, politics, and entertainment. They don't even mean "fly-over people" to be a particularly demeaning description, although of course it is. It's their way of trying to define the middle of the country as a market. As in, "The script for this movie reads well, but how do you think it will play with the fly-over people?"

What they don't understand—what they will probably never understand—is that some of us like being the people who are flown over. Because if you are a fly-over person, you by definition have your feet on the ground. It's one of the inherent qualities that comes with choosing to live in the heart of the country.

This book you are holding in your hands celebrates the Midwest, tries to explain what it is and what it means and why that matters. Never mind that the national politicians seem to awaken to the values of the Midwest only once every four years, when they start adding up the electoral votes they'll need; never mind that the film producers in Los Angeles think about us only when they're trying to come up with scenic backgrounds that speak of long days and honest work and endless horizons. That's all right; we who live here—even when we have the opportunities to live somewhere else, to live among the people who fly over people like us—stay here because we understand there's no place in the world that feels as right.

You breathe easier here. That's a simple way to put it—a brief way to sum up tangled and complex emotions—but it's accurate and it's real. There aren't a lot of starmakers in the Midwest—not a lot of talent agents hustling to turn someone on every corner into a celebrity. To be noticed by the outside world, you've got to be just a little better, try just a little harder, be just a little truer to who you are than if you lived on the East or West coasts. You don't run with the pack because there is no pack. The voice you hear—the voice telling you the way to pursue your dreams—is your own.

And you trust it, just as you trust the Midwest itself. No matter how far you travel—how many of the world's fabled nations you touch down in—you always end up coming back here. People can spend their whole lives flying over places, but when it's time to land they land back in the Midwest, because there's no other place on the globe that has ever been better able to fill that most essential role: Home.

Bob Greene

WHO ARE THOSE FARMERS ANYWAY?

The cover art is titled *American Gothic* and was painted in 1930 by Grant Wood.

You may have heard:

- The painting insults farmers and all Midwesterners by mocking their simplicity and seriousness.

- The painting portrays a married couple.

- The building in the background is a church.

The truth is:

- Grant intended the people to be seen as being from a small town, not as farmers; he felt the man's shirt indicated this. He wanted to create people who were "American Gothic," to match the window they had in their home, and he didn't see them as coming from any specific place in the country. He was upset that people were insulted by it. One of his comments on the painting was,

  > There is satire in American Gothic, but only as there is satire in any realistic statement. These are types of people I have known all my life. I tried to characterize them truthfully—to make them more like themselves than they were in actual life. They had their bad points, and I did not paint these under, but to me, they were basically good and solid people. I had no intentions of holding them up to ridicule. (*My Brother, Grant Wood*, p. 77)

- The subjects in the painting portrayed a father and daughter. The models were Grant's dentist, Dr. Byron McKeeby, and Grant's younger sister, Nan. The two never posed together for the painting.

- The building in the background is a house in Eldon, Iowa. It was donated to the State Historical Society but is usually rented to a private party.

Of further interest:

- American Gothic is said to be the second most parodied painting in the world, after *Mona Lisa*.

- Grant painted the picture at a time when women wore their hair with ironed waves, and Nan had to agree to comb hers straight while she posed.

- Grant asked Nan to locate rickrack, which she had to rip from an old dress of her mother's. His use of rickrack in this painting brought a revival for the decoration that lasted well into the 1950s.

- Gertrude Stein loved it and pronounced Grant to be America's foremost artist.

- Grant Wood was born in 1892 in Anamosa, Iowa, and died in Iowa City, Iowa, in 1942.

Where We Came From

In the Midwest, climate, soil, and food—
these three preconditions to a flourishing civilization—
are favourable.

– Alfred North Whitehead (1861–1947)

If you put your fingers lightly on a globe so that they rest near, say, Bismarck, North Dakota, and Omaha, Nebraska, and then, holding your fingers still, slowly twirl the globe to Europe and western Asia, your fingers would rest on or near the countries whose emigrants settled the Midwest in the 1800s. Now, of course, Midwesterners are "from" every country whose citizens have come to the United States. Some have been here a few years, others for five generations or more.

The immigrants came for the land, the homesteading, the railroad building, the fur trapping, the buffalo killings, or the town building—one, two, three generations altering a landscape, coming not as visitors but as settlers, to make new and prosperous lives for themselves.

Ethnic groups often settled together. The familiarity of language, religion, and ways of living eased their "replacement." Thus, the Germans landed in Wisconsin and Iowa, and the Scandinavians went farther north. Many of the Irish, Greeks, and Italians stayed in the cities; Chicago is a testament to this phenomenon.

Integration of all these groups has not always been easy. And because of the nature of America or perhaps the nature of people, it never will be simple. But it comes. There are few places left where the Finns are nervous about the Swedes next door. And it is common for American children, now the results of generations of ethnic intermarriages, to say what they "are" by naming ancestry groups on their fingers like favorite foods. But the effects of the early settlers—their customs, their hard work, their food preparation, their construction methods, their values, and their expectations all lay across the land like layers of air for the next generation to breathe.

But what caused early settlers to leave their homelands? Sometimes it was escape from overpopulation—several European countries were simply crowded. In the countries that now comprise Germany, for example, land had passed down and been divided among generations of families until the portions were not large enough to support the people trying to live on them. Seasons of poor crops caused more problems, and no amount of hard work could compensate for the losses. Such difficulties were one reason for leaving. A longing for freedom of speech or religion inspired others. Most often, people moved then for the same reason they move now—hope for a better life.

Promoters who worked for the railroads sent literature to European towns promising the elements of a wonderful life—free or cheap land, fertile soil, plentiful game, and lots of forest. There was certainly truth to the promise, but sometimes it was a smaller truth than the publicity suggested.

Even letters from friends or relatives who had emigrated earlier were a mix of myth and reality. But nevertheless, people came. They came by the thousands, so that America found itself tumbling west, every decade a witness to amazing growth in population as the frontier was pushed yet another hundred miles away from the Atlantic Ocean. And growth in the Midwest was not simply from immigrants arriving by boat. Many immigrants who first settled in upstate New York, for example, moved on to Kentucky or Ohio, and then to Indiana and on perhaps to Minnesota or Illinois. Many of those who ultimately moved to the Midwest had settled farther east first and then decided to strike out for the less settled areas.

Books published at the time told travelers both what to bring and what to expect. And once the restless urge came upon one family in a village, it wasn't uncommon for neighbors to become inspired by the same dream and decide to go along. Entire villages sometimes packed up their belongings to embark on the New World adventure.

Of course, not everyone in the Midwest is rooted to the settlers from the nineteenth century. There were those who lived here before—Native American tribes and early French trappers—and there are those who are still coming. Today, we share this space and the varied heritage that makes us all Midwesterners.

Who Was Here First

Before prairies bloomed, the Midwest soil grew ancient forests and was home to prehistoric animals and insects, including—about 260 million years ago—a spry-looking cockroach-like insect that was close to a foot long. And 120 million years before that, ocean covered the territory, and fish the size of modern sharks swam above the Midwest. But the water gave way to dry land and forests, which eventually gave way to prairies.

And prior to the tribes whose names are known to us today, the Midwest was peopled by hunters and gatherers as well as people who cultivated crops. Before the Europeans came, midwestern inhabitants lived without wheels and without horses, both of which can ease physical labor and provide improved transportation. We all know how much ten years can change an area; here are a few snapshots from the past thousands of years.

● ● ●

Twin Ditch Site, Illinois, is the location of the **oldest house** in the Midwest. Archaeologists date it from 9,500 years ago. Talk about calling the Midwest home.

Near Jeffers, Minnesota, you can view **two thousand prehistoric petroglyphs** of holy figures, people, turtles, deer, and other animals. The carvings are in an exposed ridge of red quartzite bedrock and were made between 3000 B.C. and 500 A.D.

The Mound-Builders is a name given to thousands of people in scores of tribes who lived in the middle of the continent from about 3000 B.C. to 500 A.D. All of these early groups built mounds—sometimes for burial and sometimes for

The most populous ethnic groups in Kansas are Germans, English, and Irish.

worship. Wisconsin has **12,000 Indian mounds.** One of the most unusual is a relief of a man walking, which is near Baraboo at Man Mound Park; it measures 210 feet by forty-seven feet. In Illinois, near East St. Louis, is Monks Mound, a truncated pyramid that rises more than one hundred feet from ground level. The Great Serpent Mound in Adams City, Ohio, is 1,330 feet long and averages three feet in height.

A dugout canoe was **found in a peat bog** in Ashland County, Wisconsin, in 1977. It was estimated to date from about 1600 B.C., older than any other known water vehicle in this part of the world.

In May 1994, the construction of a freeway and the necessary moving of muck unearthed some **surprisingly large teeth.** It turned out that they had belonged to a mastodon who had wandered the area some 14,000 years prior. We have all kinds of interesting "ghosts" in our past.

The infants of Native Americans had to be quiet in order for their parents to hunt game and to **guard against enemies.** Parents held the noses of crying babies or placed them away from family and activity to teach them this critical skill.

Moss or the cotton-like seed heads of cattails placed in babies' cradleboards did the duty of modern diapers. **More biodegradable** than anything on the market today.

Tribal plainsmen hunted and killed the buffalo, and the women slaughtered it, prepared it for cooking, and found uses for the **bones and hide.**

Kansas peacemakers included Wild Bill Hickok, Bat Masterson, and Wyatt Earp.

Tribal children learned to bathe every day, summer and winter, usually in nearby streams or pools. Since there was **no hot water,** a cold water bath was taken for granted. Doesn't it make you feel spoiled?

Tribal families never grew too large because many children died in their first few years of life, and mothers died giving birth, too. Their **custom of community care** of the children helped in those times. Extended members of the family lived together, too, which provided support, as we would say in current jargon.

Children were encouraged to become skilled in adult activities. They were given small bows and arrows, and **dolls made of pine needles** or other vegetation.

Many tribes built homes to hold several families. This is evidenced by both the portable tepees and the permanent adobe houses. Children learned when they were young to play in **their own space** and respect the invisible boundaries that marked the territory of others.

The most populous ethnic groups in Illinois are Germans, Irish, and Polish.

Church Membership in the Midwest

The range of the most common religious affiliations of Midwesterners links to the countries whose emigrants came in vast numbers to settle the area. Although these groups have the largest memberships, there are hundreds of belief systems represented in the midwestern states including: African, Pentecostal, Apostolic, Reformed, Baha'i, Buddhist, Congregational, Latter Day Saints, Mennonite, Amish, Orthodox, Muslim, Presbyterian, and New Age.

CATHOLICS	13,799,181
LUTHERANS	4,393,771
BAPTISTS	1,708,306
METHODISTS	1,304,592
UNITED CHURCH OF CHRIST	865,905
JEWISH	666,128
ASSEMBLY OF GOD	411,673
EPISCOPALIANS	330,581

Of Midwesterners who attend church, the greatest proportion of membership is among Catholics. This is true for every state with the exception of North and South Dakota, where Lutherans dominate. Lutherans run a close second to Catholics in Minnesota (24.2 percent and 25.4 percent), and in Missouri, Southern Baptist convention members are nearly as plentiful as Roman Catholics (15.4 percent and 15.7 percent).

Aren't you learning a lot?

The Native American population in South Dakota is 50,000.

How We Love to Move!

Why did people in early America move so much? Historians cite both economic and cultural reasons. David M. Potter pushes the idea to the point where it seems un-American if you didn't move. In his book, People of Plenty: Economic Abundance and the American Character, *Potter writes: "In a country where the entire environment was to be transformed with the least possible delay, a man who was not prepared to undergo personal transformation was hardly an asset. Hence, mobility became not merely an optional privilege, but almost a mandatory obligation, and the man who failed to meet this obligation had, to a certain extent, defaulted in his duty to society."*

Tom Lincoln brought his family from Kentucky in 1816 to Little Pigeon Creek in old Perry—now Spencer—County, Indiana. His family, of course, included his wife, Nancy, and their children, Sarah, nine, and Abraham, seven. Imagine **Abraham Lincoln at seven.**

Following this midwestern tradition of moving around, the **first White settlers** in South Dakota were farmers from Wisconsin, Minnesota, and Iowa, many of whom had come from New York, New England, and Pennsylvania. Eventually thousands more moved to the state from Norway, Sweden, Denmark, Germany, Russia, Czechoslovakia, Hungary, Holland, Ireland, Scotland, Finland, and Poland. In the 1870s and 1880s a few hundred moved in from the other direction when Chinese came from California. Moving seems to be deep in our genes. And that makes all those moving companies very happy.

Ohio was home to Shawnee, Erie, Miami, Delaware, and Wyandot (Huron) tribes.

But as fast as people moved in, they moved out. **In 1840 Ohio lost more people than it gained** and in the 1850s, so did Indiana.

Dr. William Mayo, of Mayo Clinic fame, was a classic Midwesterner in his reluctance to settle. At age twenty-five, he traveled from England to New York City, then moved on to Buffalo (where he was a tailor), to Missouri, to Indiana, and then to Minnesota. Even there, he moved from LeSeuer to Rochester to Minneapolis. **His wife stopped moving** once they'd settled in Rochester in 1864. Mayo traveled to Minneapolis for a while to work at the medical school, but when his wife refused to follow, saying enough was enough, especially with a new baby, Mayo moved back to Rochester and stayed.

In 1860, **less than one-third of the heads of households** in Ohio had been born there. In Illinois that year, the figure was less than eight percent.

The importance to settlers of maintaining their culture is not to be overlooked. In his book, *Sugar Creek: Life on the Illinois Prairie,* John Mack Faragher, says that the settlers of that town "transported a traditional social order to a new environment and had **progressively transformed the landscape** in ways compatible with their own priorities. . . . Family and household remained the essential social building blocks; community continued to be constructed from the relations among kinships, neighborhood, and church."

While people have been emptying the rural areas and moving into the cities for several generations, this long-standing trend has begun to change. According to a recent study, the "non-metro" counties experienced growth in the early 1990s and even more is expected. City-dwellers are apparently finding that the suburbs are not far enough out to escape so-called urban ills. It seems that people are looking for what is offered by a small-town atmosphere, plus good recreation. **Nostalgia plus aerobics,** I guess, which is not the same as aerobic nostalgia, a condition known only to owners of Jane Fonda's first work-out video.

Early settlers made ink by boiling black walnut shells.

Who Came

If there were marked paths to the Midwest that began at every new-comer's homeland and followed him or her to the new homestead, you'd see dotted lines leading all around the world.

A million Swedes—when Sweden's population was seven million—emigrated to the U.S. between 1840 and 1880.

Most Germans came because of testimonials from friends and relatives that arrived via what came to be called **"America Letters."** Also, various German organizations sent representatives to scout the area in America and send reports back home.

The ethnic variety that was so dramatic for settlers a century ago in the Midwest has **melded together** in the eyes of the census takers, so that now "white" covers most of them. South Dakota, a largely white state is, nevertheless, fourth nationally in its population of Native Americans.

Concentrations of Dutch populations can be found in Holland, Michigan; Oostburg, Wisconsin; Greenleafton, Minnesota; and Pella and Orange City, Iowa. If all of the soil displaced by all the **thousands of tulip bulbs** in those towns were gathered together, you might build yourself a heckuva hill, maybe the size of Mount Rushmore. A lot of bulbs, a lot of dirt.

Most families owned one cheap clock by the 1830s.

In addition to well-known ethnic groups, some immigrants are from less well-known groups, one being the Samit, or as others have identified them, the Lapps. They are indigenous to the northern parts of Norway, Sweden, Finland, and Russia, in an area named Lapland; most of them used to be **semi-nomadic.** As is not uncommon for nomadic peoples, the Samit were discriminated against by some, and, as early immigrants, they often felt they had to keep their ethnic identity a secret. A quarterly newsletter is published by the group in Duluth.

A book called *Hints to Immigrants* advised early travelers that a family could **start life in the New World with about 150 dollars** if they farmed. The book suggested the purchase of cleared land between forty-one and thirty-seven degrees latitude.

The **first White immigrant** in Wisconsin was Ole Knutson Nattestad from Norway. He settled in what would become Jefferson Prairie in Rock County. His brother brought more Norwegians, and that was the beginning of that.

In England, only the oldest son could **inherit land.** That inspired some emigration.

Recent immigrants to America—and there are many in the Midwest—include the Hmong people. Wisconsin is home to **7,500 Hmong,** the third largest concentration in the nation, after Minnesota and California. Puj Ntaub—pronounced pon dow—is the bold-colored needlework done by Hmong women that has recently become an American craft.

Villa Louis, a mansion-turned-museum in Prairie du Chien, Wisconsin, commemorates the area's **earliest days of fur-trading.** The owner of the magnificent home was Hercules Dousman, who made his fortune with beaver pelts and railroads.

The most populous ethnic groups in Michigan are Germans, English, and Irish.

Germans immigrated to America by the thousands, many to escape the political and economic upheaval in that part of the world during the last century. Germans had strong feelings of **loyalty toward their homeland,** but like many other immigrants they wanted their hard work to mean something. Most who came paid their own way, but sometimes town councils raised the needed travel funds for an indigent who wanted to emigrate to America.

Those who sought **religious freedom** usually assimilated more slowly into the new country than those who came for economic improvement.

Frankenmuch, Michigan, was settled in the 1840s by Germans. One of the ways the town retains its Old World sensibility is by the hourly playing of a **thirty-five-bell glockenspiel,** a large version of the bell lyre you've seen in marching bands. I'll bet tourists raise their eyebrows over that.

Michigan's 1850 population was almost **fifty times its 1820 population,** which was about nine thousand.

The 1990 census of county populations lists the numbers of people who claim "first ancestry" among those **classified now as "White."** Nationalities included are: Czech, Danish, Dutch, English, French, French Canadian, German, Greek, Hungarian, Irish, Italian, Norwegian, Polish, Portuguese, Russian, Scotch-Irish, Scottish, Slovak, Swedish, Swiss, and Welsh.

Prairie schooner was the nickname for covered wagons with their billowed tops.

Julien Dubuque was Iowa's first White settler, but unlike a lot of "first" settlers, his name is still known and not just for the historically **rich river town.** There was also that wise crack by *New Yorker* editor Harold Ross about not wanting to edit a magazine for "the old lady from Dubuque." I wonder how many Dubuquers subscribe to the magazine.

Josiah and Abigail Snelling not only gave their name to Fort Snelling— **Minnesota's first fort,** later named St. Paul—but were dubbed the state's first "first family."

Indiana's 1820 census, which numbered less than 150,000 people, included over **one thousand free Black slaves.**

And how about this: **eight-six percent of recent immigrants** to the Midwest indicated in a 1995 survey that they had a better opportunity to get a job here than in their homeland. And seventy percent of them felt they could expect fair treatment under the laws.

After Kansas Territory was established in 1854, northerners hurried to populate it with **"Free-Soilers,"** and proslavery Missourians did the same with the opposite goal. (The "Free-Soilers" were part of a national political party, and the "Free-Staters" were members of a Kansan political party. The parties had the same goal; no doubt many Kansans belonged to both.)

Two **brothers from France** named La Verendrye followed the not uncommon custom of early explorers when, in 1743, they buried a carved piece of lead to further establish France's claim to what was then the Louisiana Territory. A monument now honors the men at Fort Pierre, which is across the Missouri River from Pierre, South Dakota's capital.

The most populous ethnic groups in Minnesota are Germans, Norwegians, and Swedes.

Once Upon a Time . . . But True

–from the *1884 History of Green County, Wisconsin*

On the 10th of April 1845, 193 persons of all ages and both sexes stood on the banks of the Linth canal, which runs alongside of the Linth river, a tributary of the Rhine, in the canton of Glarus in Switzerland. They had declared their readiness to venture into the strange, far-off land called America, about which they had read and heard so much. In the land they were leaving, poverty stared them in the face, with no hope of improvement. Before them lay the land of golden promise, where, they believed, honest labor would meet its just reward and they could lift themselves and their children to competence, independence, and equality with others.

The group proceeded to Rotterdam, Holland, and waited while the ship was fitted to carry passengers. They departed May 19th and arrived in Baltimore forty-nine days later—"a stormy, toilsome voyage."

From there, the group took a train to Columbia, Pennsylvania, then transferred to a canal boat that ferried them to Pittsburgh. Barges carried them to Cincinnati, Ohio, and steamboats transported them to St. Louis, Missouri, where they arrived July 23rd. Swiss countrymen met them there, and they settled in temporarily while two of their men went north.

The advance men went to Galena, Illinois, and were then guided to Mineral Point, Wisconsin, over "trackless country for thirty-two miles" using a compass. They sent word back to St. Louis for the immigrants to come along.

By the 15th of August the main body of immigrants had arrived,

In 1900, 34% of Wisconsin's population was German.

and a large shelter had been built. Short of food, they had to rely on the stream. And also short on hooks and lines, they divided the work so some caught bait—grasshoppers—and others caught fish. The men had brought their axes and building tools of all kinds, and the women had brought pots and kettles and utensils. Thus began New Glarus, Wisconsin, a town that sank its roots deep and continues to thrive.

And now a word from one of our own. . .

Two Grandmothers

One lost, never known,
Nine children she bore
And died with the last.
The other I knew—
She crossed the Atlantic at three
And died in protest at ninety-six.
"Death was," she would say,
"Uncalled for."
She could card wool and spin it,
And knit toe *and heel.*
She could cook potatoes
Eight ways at least
And believed any illness would yield
To eucalyptus tea, and brandy.

— Eugene McCarthy, Senator and Presidential Candidate
Reprinted from *Gene McCarthy's Minnesota: Memories of a Native Son,* 1982.

The growth rate in Michigan from 1820 to 1830 was 537.15%.

How They Traveled

Moving from Europe to America or moving from the coast to inland areas was a trial that we in the Concorde jet era have a hard time truly imagining. Ships that relied on wind to cross the Atlantic took weeks and weeks to travel from one shore to the other. Settlers moving to the Middle West from the East by covered wagon tried to plan their journey for early spring so that they would have time to plant and harvest at least a small crop to help them survive the winter. We drive the stretch in a marathon day knowing that there's always fast food available.

● ● ●

The railroad movement transformed the Midwest. In 1850, for example, the Illinois Central Railroad received the first federal land grant to build a railbed. Their "prize" was over 250,000 acres along the track, where, of course, major development occurred. The 705-mile stretch from Chicago to Cairo, Illinois, was completed in 1856. **The Cannonball Express,** saved by Casey Jones in life as well as in song, was an Illinois Central train.

With apologies to Madison County, Iowa (and Robert Waller's book on the subject): Parke County, Indiana, contains more covered bridges than any single county in the country. **Indiana claims 104 covered bridges** in its thirty-four counties. (Bridges were covered for the very practical reason of protecting the bridge itself from the elements and prolonging its usefulness.)

A steamboat trip down the Ohio River in the early 1800s that took travelers from the East into the Midwest might cost forty dollars. For those who supplied their own food and slept on the deck, a bargain fee of thirteen dollars would do the trick. An Ohio packet boat charged **twenty-five dollars to go five hundred miles** at that time. Such a boat had sleeping quarters that were actually deep shelves—six feet long and two feet wide.

The most populous ethnic groups in Missouri are Germans, Irish, and English.

Twelve was the number of oxen it took to pull a wagon of freight across nineteenth-century trails. Properly cared for, **oxen could walk two thousand miles** in a season.

Stagecoach etiquette included advice, such as: Spit on the leeward side of the coach, don't swear or smoke a pipe early in the morning, don't lop onto your neighbor while sleeping, don't discuss politics or religion, and don't point out locations where horrible murders took place, especially if women are present.

Fountain City, Indiana, was known as the "Grand Central Station of the Underground Railroad." Many residents allowed slaves to sleep or eat there as they made their escape to the North. **One famous Quaker couple,** Katie and Levi Coffin, estimated that they had provided overnight lodging for over two thousand fugitive slaves. One of them was Eliza, who became the heroine in Harriet Beecher Stowe's antislavery novel, *Uncle Tom's Cabin.*

By the end of the nineteenth century, owning a Pullman car for personal travel symbolized **the epitome of success in America.** Every industrialist had one, as did wise families of the socially elite. Has that translated to the RVs that plentifully and democratically sprinkle our national highways and campsites? Or should we look to Lear jets as the modern substitute?

From 1854 until 1929, the Children's Aid Society, founded by New Yorker Charles Brace, was responsible for sending **thousands of orphaned children** by train to homes on farms and in small communities in the Midwest. Andrew Burke, who grew up to become governor of North Dakota, had come west on an orphan train.

A journey by covered wagon was considered short if it was under 50 days.

The trip from Europe to America took eight weeks by sailing ship. People usually took their own food, which may have included potatoes—first boiled and then dried in a hot oven, dried fish, milk boiled with sugar and stored in sealed bottles, dried fruits, yeast and flour, and **freshly made gingerbread.** Fresh water was rationed daily, and each family was assigned a time to use a stove.

Early stagecoaches, which traveled about five miles per hour, teetered so precariously on the rutted dirt roads that it wasn't uncommon for the driver to yell instructions for the gentlemen to lean one direction or the other to keep the coach upright. Taking a stagecoach west probably meant stopping at taverns for the night, where one would often find two sleeping rooms, one for men and one for women. **Strangers frequently had to sleep in the same bed.**

In order for a covered wagon to survive the trip west, it had to be riveted together, rather than assembled with nuts and bolts, and the box, or body of the wagon, needed to be sealed against the numerous river crossings. A well-prepared family packed tools for building and planting, kitchen utensils, pots, food, **guns and ammunition.** A useful side effect of a day's bumpy ride in a covered wagon was that milk stored in a leather bag would "churn" itself into butter.

Messages were written on **the bones of buffalo** or other animals and left along the trail for future travelers to read.

The most populous ethnic groups in Indiana are Germans, English, and Irish.

Chimney Rock, Nebraska, was **a strange phenomenon** as well as a landmark for those who took a wagon train through southern Nebraska. Because of the slow pace of travel, the monolith could be seen for three weeks before it was finally passed.

Ferries were a necessary part of the trip West. In a two-week period in the fall of 1846, 582 wagons were **ferried across the Mississippi** at Burlington, Iowa.

Traveling by rail offered customers several benefits, including less bruising than in stagecoaches, and passenger cars that were heated with wood stoves and lighted with kerosene lamps. And, of course, railroads increased the speed of travel substantially, but riders had to risk the possibilities of derailments, collapsing bridges, or **head-on collisions.** The risk of nasty consequences doesn't often prevent us from seeking comfort, though, does it?

One of the most remarkable treks west is known as the Handcart Brigade that took place from 1856–1860 by the Mormons. A handcart is similar to a Chinese rickshaw except that the carrying section is an open box for household goods. Approximately **three thousand people of all ages** pulled or walked alongside these carts for 1,300 miles as they crossed prairies, rivers, and mountains on their way to Utah.

Ohio's population was 45,000 in 1800 and 231,000 in 1810.

Naming Our Towns

Towns were named in any number of ways—sometimes by where people had come from, sometimes to reflect the hope of new settlers, and sometimes by what people longed for. Beatrice, Nebraska, is a case in point for the last reason; it was settled by men who missed women. When a woman named Beatrice came to town, the men were inspired to name the town for her. I don't know how she reacted. Perhaps with a blush. Here are a few naming tales from Iowa and elsewhere.

• • •

One town was given the wrong—or at least an unplanned—name. It was to be called Harmon after a man who had been a pioneer there. A speech was prepared, a platform erected, and a ceremony planned. The townspeople assembled. But the speaker had been reading **Sir Walter Scott** and was apparently so distracted by the tale that when he was supposed to declare the name of the new town, he said instead, "Now I pronounce the name of this town, Waverly." (The title of the book that so absorbed him was *Waverley*.) Thus, Waverly, Iowa, it became, and home of Wartburg College, too. Oh, my.

Another town's name resulted from an out-and-out bribe. An Ohio judge traveling with his daughter in Iowa agreed to buy land in the town if they would name it after his daughter, Exira. So they did. Yes, **that was a bribe** and a judge in the same story.

Sometimes women got involved accidentally in the naming of towns. One such case was the town of Lemars, Iowa, which doesn't sound like a woman's name and it's not. People haggled and haggled and couldn't agree until someone suggested they take the first letters of **the town's six prettiest girls'** names and construct a word. They came up with Lemars. I'm not sure if such creativity should be commended or not.

The Dakotah (often called Sioux) Indians lived in the upper Midwest. Some still do.

An Easterner named John Blair was the chief promoter and builder of the Chicago & Northwestern Railroads. Before he died, he ran seventeen railroads. As the laying of tracks kept progressing into the West, he had a heyday naming towns. A good friend of his was Oaks Ames, and so: Ames, home to Iowa State University. Blair then named a town after his daughter, Alta—a nice thing to do, except that Alta had a sister, Aurelia, who was very envious. So Blair did what any good father would do and named another town Aurelia. Then one day, his dog died. **The dog was named Colo,** so now there's a Colo, Iowa. Finally, he realized he had no town named after himself, so he named Blair, Iowa, in his own honor. I guess that felt good because then he proceeded to name Blairsburg, Iowa, and as the tracks went into Nebraska, he named Blair, Nebraska, for himself, too. Perhaps that was enough, because some people who wanted the railroad to go through their city, named it Blair City to attract his attention, but it didn't work.

Big Whiskey Creek and Little Whiskey Creek, both in Iowa, were named for **whiskey that was buried there** at the time. It's probably long gone.

Once it was believed that Topeka, Kansas, was named after **a tribal word for potato.** But that was wrong. You have to wonder why people would want to name a town "potato" anyway.

Covered wagons pulled by oxen traveled about 4 miles per day.

Frontier Settlers

My four grandparents came to the United States shortly after the Civil War from what was then called Bohemia, although my maternal grandparents came from Moravia, part of the Czech region. Germany was the protectorate of both regions.

They came over in steerage. It was the era when railroads were sponsoring cheap passages to increase the population along their lines. I think they were headed for the West Coast, but the train was derailed in Nebraska. The railroad offered them a cash settlement for their minor injuries. They took it and both families settled in Saunders County.

My mother's father dug a sod house into the side of a prominent hill. It had a door and two windows in front. My mother said it was quite comfortable—cool in the summer, warm in the winter. The floors were dirt, but hard as concrete due to constant use. They had a large iron kitchen range which was used for cooking and heating. After a torrential rain, the roof sometimes leaked and an occasional frog or snake might drop from the ceiling.

My grandfather was a musician in Bohemia and continued to ply his trade in small Nebraska communities. He had a large illustrated Czech Bible which he read to the family. My grandmother had to constantly remind him not to neglect his farm work.

When my mother was born, she was pronounced dead by the midwife. My grandfather placed her on a bench behind the range usually reserved for cats and wood, and he went to the barn to build her a coffin. In the morning, my grandmother said, "Let me see that baby once more before you nail the lid down." They were astonished to see

More than 200,000 men from Indiana fought for the North in the Civil War.

my mother blinking up at them. Heat from the stove apparently revived her. She lived to be seventy-five and bore eleven children.

When my mother was five or six, she was playing in the dirt road that ran past their farm. She heard cookware banging, horses snorting, and dogs barking a short distance away. Indians were coming from the nearby reservation. Three or four of them galloped toward the terrified child. My grandmother grabbed a shotgun from the corner and dashed out to confront the Indians. She shouted at them in Czech. They answered in Pawnee. Soon tired of arguing, the horsemen dashed through my grandmother's garden and took off down the road, much to grandma's and my mother's relief.

And those were the tales I heard as I was growing up about my roots in Nebraska.

James Vondra, Sr.
Born in 1911
Omaha, Nebraska

The most populous ethnic groups in Nebraska are Germans, Irish, and English.

How They Lived

The early settlers lived with a lot of risks. The weather, the animals, the Native tribespeople (when they didn't get along), the availability or scarcity of food, water, and fuel all contributed to daily lives that held a lot of uncertainties. To live such lives called for both hardiness and adaptability. And that's probably an understatement.

• • •

Homes for early pioneers differed depending upon which resource was available. In the eastern Midwest, **plentiful timber** was sawed and log cabins were assembled first. In the western Midwest, prairie was cut and sod houses were often the first home.

A typical sod house measured fourteen by eighteen feet and was built into a slope. The placement helped it stay **warm in the winter and cool in the summer.** Smoke escaped through a hole in the roof, and, after a few months of use, the dirt floor grew hard. Despite the virtues of sod houses, most homesteaders were eager to build a home of wood.

Snakes were plentiful on the plains and considered as pesky as mice are today. Pioneer women, who were not surprised to find snakes invading their parlors or yards (which doesn't necessarily mean it was a ho-hum experience), generally killed them, sometimes with sticks, sometimes with their bare hands. Early cabins were sometimes lined with bleached muslin. Although attractive, the muslin provided an **ideal resting place for snakes.** A settler who spotted a moving roll would spear the snake with a pitchfork, loosen the muslin, and remove the snake. Fall housecleaning often turned up more of the reptiles— in the rafters, hiding within furniture, or even inside the pump organ. A whole new reason to postpone housecleaning.

The first permanent settlement by Whites in Ohio took place in Mariette in 1794.

On the frontier, people made their own candles, soap, and maple sugar, and wove and sewed their own clothes. Salt had to be imported. **A bushel of alum salt was worth a cow and a calf.**

In the mid-1800s, the Kiowa, Comanche, and Arapahoe tribes were so fed up with treaties, land allotments, and government rations that they raided wagon trains for over a year. The effect was a severe reduction in available goods. The price of a sack of flour in Colorado and New Mexico rose to forty-five dollars. Other typical prices of the time included **bacon at twenty-five cents per pound,** a handkerchief at one dollar, a vest for five dollars, a man's shirt at three dollars, and a pound of tobacco for one dollar. A good example of pure supply and demand.

The Walnut Creek Massacre occurred around the mid-1800s in Kansas. About 125 tribesmen attacked a wagon train that was within view of Camp Dunlap, which was being manned by fewer than a hundred volunteer soldiers (the regulars were deeply engaged around the Potomac in the Civil War). Captain Dunlap headed out with his men to aid the travelers but then, terrified, he turned and **hightailed it back to the fort.** Ten men from the wagon train were killed. Two teen-agers, Robert McGee of Easton, Kansas, and Allen W. Edwards, Iowa, who were wounded and scalped, managed to survive. The graves of the dead—one with eight White men and one with two African-Americans—were discovered in April 1973, after a Walnut Creek flood had receded.

A puncheon floor, often found in frontier homes, was **an improvement over dirt floors.** It was created by laying split logs next to each other. Sometimes they were smoothed somewhat with an ax or hatchet.

The Midwest has approximately 19.6% of the U.S. population.

Home on the Range

-from the history of Kearny County, Kansas

A PIONEER NAMED Mrs. Bugbee, who had lived in her "commodious dugout" on the banks of the Arkansas River for a few years with her husband, Thomas, decided to celebrate the growing number of neighbors in Kansas by hosting a Christmas dinner. It would be the kind she used to have in Missouri.

After placing the table at its full length in their one-room home, she opened the boxes and barrels of her precious linen, china, and silver. Her mother, who still lived in Missouri, had sent a fruit cake six weeks earlier, and this delectable treat, decorated with a few holly leaves, adorned the center of the table.

Thomas took the buggy to town to pick up the guests, and Mrs. Bugbee basted her roasting antelope one more time. She was suddenly startled by a heavy rumbling noise overhead, accompanied by the sound of ripping ceiling paper and clumps of dirt falling onto the table. She looked out to see an immense buffalo standing in front of her door. The animal had tramped across her roof, stabbing holes with its hooves as it went.

Mrs. Bugbee was so furious that she picked up a gun and shot the animal. It dropped dead, right at the front door, and not until her husband and guests arrived, could it be dragged out of the way. When the path was cleared, the hostess greeted her guests, who took the event in good spirits, and a festive dinner was enjoyed by all.

The Chippewa was the fourth-largest tribe in the U.S. between 1800 and 1934.

The Chicago Expansion

The Great Migration is the name given to the brief era, which began in 1917, when African-Americans moved to northern cities. Thousands of Blacks came to Chicago, Illinois, to take advantage of the jobs that had opened up because of World War I. They were immensely relieved to earn more than they had on farms in the South. They were also often surprised to realize that they could register to vote and that Black and White children attended the same school.

Among the problems inevitable with so many coming to the city so fast was housing. Unlike the prairie settlers who could use their own tools to erect a sod hut until they could build a wooden house, Blacks moving into Chicago lived with friends and relatives until they could find and afford their own homes. Unfortunately, landlords often charged up to fifty percent more for rent from their Black tenants than they asked from their White ones.

Preceding the Great Migration, about 50,000 Blacks lived in integrated neighborhoods on Chicago's south side. The first four years of the expansion, 1917 to 1921, brought another 50,000 to the area, and by 1930, over 200,000 people had moved in. That kind of growth demands high-powered urban planning, and there had been none. Instead there was rapid adaptation. It was the beginning of another change in Chicago's population, just as there had been changes with each new wave of immigration.

The largest ethnic groups in North Dakota are Germans, Norwegians, and Irish.

Settling In

We shouldn't underestimate the grave difficulties involved in moving to a new land with only raw resources at hand. A trip back to the homeland for a visit was a rare event. Instead, people figured out how to cope. And I don't think there was a lot of talk about anyone's "inner child."

• • •

An estimated **889,000 letters** traveled from the U.S. to Holland in the decade between 1820 and 1830. That is remarkable, but then it was letters or nothing—no faxes, no dime-a-minute calls on the weekends, no beaming satellites.

John Brown, fervid abolitionist and **father of twenty,** engaged in anti-slavery activities across the Midwest, from Ohio where he worked for the Underground Railroad to Kansas where his fame turned to infamy. Heeding a divine call, he and seven others murdered five settlers whom they believed to be pro-slavery. Brown's exploits ended at Harper's Ferry in 1859 when the arsenal he and his band had occupied was recaptured by Colonel Robert E. Lee. Brown was hung, thereby becoming a martyr to the antislavery cause. "John Brown's Body" was probably the most popular Union song during the Civil War.

Talk about homesick. The people of Elk Horn, Iowa, apparently missed their Danish roots and decided to do something about it. In 1976, they **had a windmill shipped to them,** piece by piece—30,000 in all. The heaviest, no doubt, was the two-thousand-pound stone used for grinding. The windmill works, by the way.

Indiana's rate of growth was 455.47% between 1810 and 1820.

The early Midwest had certain traits because of its newness and its vastness. Some historians said the area developed with more social and economic democracy because of the **abundance of land;** there was greater equality of opportunity because there was always more room and more resources. Yet, with all that space, it was possible to flout laws. The shortage of judges and jails contributed to another early midwestern element: vigilantism.

Charles Dickens reported his own view of life along the Ohio River when he traveled America in the 1830s. He said that he saw "a road that was perfectly alive with **pigs of all ages;** lying about in every direction, fast asleep; or grunting along in quest of hidden dainties."

South Dakota's timeline shows a hundred years of activity by varied interests. The Gold Rush in the Black Hills, late in the nineteenth century, displaced the tribes. Then ranchers seized **large tracts of land.** They, of course, were moved aside though not away by homesteaders. Now farmers and ranchers are both facing possible expulsion as the Dakotas are talked about as a feasible site for the nation's garbage dump or a new buffalo commons.

Most settlers had to rely on improvised time pieces. Many of them pounded sticks into the ground to make **crude sun dials.** To time baking, they marked candles for specific lengths of time.

Early farmers harvested their crops with sickles and scythes. Cutting off the stalks or grains by hand was slow, **hard work,** but since the fields in many areas were studded with tree stumps or rocks, the method was practical for the times.

Less efficient for light but commonly used in frontier homes was a "cruisie"— a wick of linen cloth protruding from **a shallow dish of lard.** A somewhat brighter light was made by dipping the pith of cattails in lard and letting it harden. These were called rushlights and were both smelly and smoky. Another reminder of the joy of the lightswitch.

The most populous ethnic groups in Ohio are Germans, Irish, and English.

Early settlers kept **sheep for wool,** which they carded, spun, wove into cloth, dyed perhaps, and sewed into clothing. Other fabric was purchased from the peddler during his periodic rounds or during an infrequent trip to a town.

A Mrs. Carrie David, who moved to Lakin, Nebraska, from the Shenendoah Valley in Virginia in the 1870s **longed for elm trees.** She ordered some elms and cottonwoods for her home, but soon learned there was insufficient rain for the trees and no practical way to water them. The manager of the local Harvey Eating House solved her problem by offering to purchase them. The trees were planted around a fountain in front of the building, and although the cotton-woods failed, the elms flourished, some of them living for decades.

Abilene, Kansas, was a cattle boom town in the mid-1800s. Longhorn cattle could be purchased in Texas for two to four dollars per head; in Abilene, they sold for twenty to forty dollars each. The Texas cattlemen who brought the steers north must have been heady with their prosperity. They were **flagrantly lawless** until a young man named Thomas J. Smith became marshal. He enforced the ordinance against carrying guns in town by punching offenders and wresting their pistols. Encouraged shopkeepers and saloon owners helped the cause by insisting that guns be "parked" until visitors left town. Smith is remembered as the man who calmed down Abilene.

The Osage tribe lived in what is now Missouri.

It is not surprising that Native American names are all over our maps. Tribal names or words from their languages are scattered across the Midwest, as they are across the country. Here are a few:

SOUTH DAKOTA
Iroquois, Huron, Oglala, Yankton

NORTH DAKOTA
Lakota, Absaraka, Mandan

MINNESOTA
Pequot Lakes, Dakota, Winnebago

WISCONSIN
Ojibwa, Kickapoo Center, Sauk City

IOWA
Iowa City, Sioux City, Ute

KANSAS
Kansas City, Wea, Wichita, Kiowa

NEBRASKA
Omaha, Otoe, Pawnee City

ILLINOIS
Illinois City, Peoria, Cahokia, Tamaroa, Kaskaskia

MICHIGAN
Fox, Menominee, Wyandotte, Erie

INDIANA
Miami, Manhattan

OHIO
Ottawa, Piqua, Bannock, Chillicothe

MISSOURI
Missouri City, Osage, Seneca

Ohio's population grew 356% between 1800 and 1810.

Before Electricity, We Made Do With . . .

KEROSENE LAMPS
We had to wash the kerosene chimneys on the lamps and only small hands fit inside. They were fragile and greasy, difficult to clean. We studied, read, and played cards or games by sitting around the table to get the best lighting possible from those small flames of light. They also provided the heat for a curling iron for my hair (and a few burnt ears!).

WINDCHARGERS
We had two tall glass batteries that charged up when the wind blew enough to make the windcharger turn. This provided some lights and accessories. They were kept in a little nook near my bedroom door. I had to be very careful as I passed them with the long skirts of the era; if they touched, I ended up with small holes near the hem from the battery acid!

COLD STORAGE
There was a tank of water in our "milk house" that was always cold. It made an excellent place to store freshly churned butter or a watermelon.

PUMPED WATER
There was no running water except from the pump. It was deliciously cold and no one worried about germs as they drank from the tin dipper. It was not much fun to carry pails of it to the house and then carry it out again in different forms! There were no ice cubes for drinks unless it was winter and then you didn't need them. I even liked "iced milk" because you had to chew part of it.

The largest ethnic groups in South Dakota are Germans, Norwegians, and English.

NOT MUCH RADIO

With the windcharger we had some radio, but it was limited according to how much wind we had. We did other things for entertainment—cards, reading, playing board games. The quiet seemed to stimulate creativity and I still prefer a quiet house when I am working.

SEPARATING CREAM FROM MILK

It was often my job to turn the handle to separate the milk from the cream. You couldn't turn it too fast or too slow or you didn't get good butterfat. Some sour cream spread on a freshly baked piece of bread with a sprinkle of sugar on it was a treat.

HANGING CLOTHES ON THE LINE

The only clothes dryer was a clothesline outside and a folding wooden dryer stand. In the winter the clothes were often 'freeze-dried' outside and had to be hung inside to finish drying. The house smelled so fresh.

COAL RANGE

The coal range had to be filled daily, for heat during winter and for cooking all year. It had a water tank on it so you had hot or lukewarm water if you kept it filled. It also provided heat for the heavy and clumsy 'sad iron' to iron our clothes.

FRESH OR HOME-CANNED FOOD

Without a refrigerator, all food was eaten fresh or canned. The Regent Coop Store had a locker where you could rent a box to store some foods, such as meat. Canned meats were delicious and the taste was unlike any prepared meat today.

Marlene Kouba
Regent, North Dakota

Midwesterners of Hispanic origin in 1990—1,726,509.

In the Middle of Things

How do we measure the middle? With globes and odometers and even with census information. Once upon a time—1790 to be exact—the middle of the U.S. was in Maryland. This middle had to do with how many people lived to the North, to the South, to the East, and to the West. The very most central person in the country was in Maryland. As more people piled onto the East Coast, that middle moved farther and farther west, until it reached its current location in Missouri, which is in the middle in other ways, too.

• • •

Not surprisingly, the **middle of the country** is "zipped" by the middle of the Zip Code: 44444 is Newton Falls, Ohio; 55555 is Young America, Minnesota (do you suppose they started there and worked east and west?); and 66666 is not yet designated, but when enough people move into a section of Kansas, it will find a home. For now, 66600 will get your mail to Topeka.

Some things to learn:

- **Rugby, North Dakota,** is the geographic center of the North American continent.

- A spot near **Lebanon, Kansas,** is the geographic center of the forty-eight contiguous states.

- After Alaska joined the Union, the geographic center of the United States (on the North American continent) **moved to a point** seventeen miles west of Castle Rock, near South Dakota's western boundary.

- A cross mark on a bronze tablet in a former corn field in the middle of Kansas is used as a survey center by the United States, Canada, and Mexico. This spot is the **geodesic center** of North America.

By 1840, Ohio had over 1,500,000 people.

Somebody with an interesting computer program figured out that one-third of all Americans **live within five hundred miles** of Wisconsin. All I can say is, if they all decide to visit, everybody in the state better put the coffee pot on.

Kansas once held the nickname **"Bleeding Kansas"** because of the battles between Free-Staters and proslavery people. The Civil War ended the controversy and the nickname.

Annie Wittenmyer from Keokuk, Iowa, established a hospital for both Confederate and Yankee soldiers after **the fall of Vicksburg**. She mobilized tremendous amounts of supplies and assistance for the men fighting the Civil War.

World War I caused many Americans to "put away" their ethnic customs. Fear, which was so prevalent, made **people want to be alike** rather than risk being different.

Menominee, Winnebago, and Potawatomi tribes lived in the northeastern Midwest.

Remembering on Decoration Day

Decoration Day in the 1950s, when I was young, was always busy for my family. For several days before the holiday, we looked for vases and jars, ribbons and bows, decided which flowers to pick, and thought about floral arrangements for the cemetery. In addition, many out-of-town relatives came to attend services at the cemetery, so there was food to prepare and baking to do.

My dad always mixed up a special white-washing solution to apply to my sister's tombstone. The tombstone would "weather" over the winter and my mom wanted it to look nice for the services. The tombstone is a life-size, white lamb in a resting position with its head up and its feet tucked under its body. I remember going with my dad to the cemetery a few days before the holiday to apply the white-wash, polish the bronze plaque, and pull away the weeds that had grown around the base of the tombstone.

In those days, only real flowers were used to decorate the cemetery. Everyone grew their own flowers and ferns for cemetery bouquets. We had to get up very early on the holiday to pick fresh flowers. Sometimes the spring weather was cold and the flowers weren't quite blooming. In that case, my mom and grandmother would cut iris and peony blooms and place their stems in buckets of warm water in the house to force them to bloom.

We made floral arrangements in vases and jars to set on the ground using metal stakes which we made from wire to prevent them from falling over. We also made floral sprays to lay on the grave sites. My mom liked to make a wreath of small flowers to put around the neck of my sister's lamb tombstone. Any extra cut flowers were also

In 1850, Iowa's population was 200,000; in 1860, more than 500,000.

taken to the cemetery and given away. It took several carloads to get all of the flowers there.

The cemetery was located out in the country, between two towns, on a small piece of farmland. There was a large metal archway and gate at the gravel road leading up the long lane to the cemetery.

On Decoration Day, my family dressed up, and someone organized a children's parade to walk throughout the cemetery, row by row. As they passed each grave, children placed American flags on veterans' graves and fresh flowers at every headstone. The children usually pulled a wagon or two loaded with the extra fresh flowers that people had brought to the cemetery.

At a set time, a local minister led the memorial service. The high school band performed. The Veterans' Honor Guard fired a twenty-one-gun salute. A trumpeter played taps. People mingled and talked to friends and family members before leaving. These activities always took place on Decoration Day (before it was called Memorial Day), regardless of the weather. When our relatives came for the services, they came home with us for a day of visiting, eating, reminiscing, and fun and games, too.

Linda Walkner Knell
Council Bluffs, Iowa

The most populous ethnic groups in Wisconsin are Germans, Polish, and Irish.

Odd Facts

"**S**cotty" Phillip, originally from Scotland, settled in South Dakota. Seeing buffalo disappear at such a rapid rate in the area inspired him to set up a buffalo ranch. The story is told of a challenge that came to him one day: A Mexican bull could make mincemeat of a buffalo.

Phillip didn't believe it. One of his buffalo was selected, and he made arrangements for it to be taken to Mexico. The animal was named **Pierre of the Plains,** and the train carrying the nearly two-thousand-pound buffalo and a few ranch hands headed south. Arriving at the designated site, the bullfight was set. But Pierre didn't understand the principles of bullfighting. Instead of charging, he defended himself as he would on the plains, by using his ability to whirl quickly on his front legs and hold his thick skull steady (these maneuvers helped to protect him from his natural enemy, the coyote). The tactics worked well to ward off the bull, which ran into him again and again, each time reacting to the shock of the impact by dropping to his knees. Four bulls were "used up" on Pierre of the Plains before the match was declared a draw. The question of which animal was the strongest apparently never came up again.

Cedar Rapids, Iowa, had a population in 1837 of one: a horse thief by the name of Osgood Shepherd. In 1838 the population swelled to five when he built a log cabin by the Cedar River and brought his wife and their two children, along with his aged father, to "settle" the town. **Times have changed,** and there are currently 108,751 residents there and not a single known horse thief among them.

Indian tribes in the eastern Midwest included the Ottawa, Illini, and Miami.

Where We Live

*When tillage begins, other arts follow. The farmers therefore
are the founders of human civilization.*

– Daniel Webster (1782–1852)

Once this land was a wide continent with a large, mysterious, and uncharted space between the oceans. Now, for people who live on either coast, the big place in the middle is often a nuisance that has to be flown *over* or, worse, has to be driven *through* to get to where they want to go.

But for many of us, the vast expanse called the Midwest, now mapped in detail and well-settled, is home. This common ground holds a familiar climate and shape, and we're used to its customs; they mean comfort to those who grew up here, even if—as kids—we couldn't wait to get out. The Midwest pervades our memories and influences our personalities—from the look of the horizon, the smell of approaching thunderstorms, and the sounds of blizzard winds to our sense of neighborhood and neighborliness—and it's something that stays with us no matter where we go.

Long ago, of course, there was no official "Midwest." When Europeans began to intrude into the area, they defined it officially as the Northwest Territory—a confusing designation, for more than a few school children—the area was north and west of lands settled by early Americans, so that's what it was called. Later, as settlers, industrialists, and entrepreneurs moved into and out of the middle of the country, we retained the "west" and gained the "mid." But where exactly, many ask, is the Midwest?

Rivers provide the easy geographical answer. A map showing the Ohio, Missouri, and Mississippi rivers and their tributaries reveals a veined shape that aligns fairly well with the Midwest. Several state boundaries followed rivers, though some were negotiated with neighboring states for borders outside of river lines. Like other regions, the Midwest is frayed along its edges—whether south, west, east or north. On the perimeter, the midwestern landscape as well as traditions and heritage blend with the characteristics of the next geographical area.

But regardless of the precision of the Midwest's borders, the central bond for the area is agriculture. Farming is what the Midwest "grew up on," and all of us, no matter what type of work we do now, are both a product of that heritage and dependent upon the continued productivity of the region. And the most tangible aspect of that productivity—the weather—is an important part of our day-to-day life. Weather has the upper hand in determining success or failure in the fields. Midwestern crops need wet times and dry times, hot times and cold times. Variety and concentration are both critical. And inasmuch as farming is the bedrock of midwestern economy, we all need and even come to long for most of what the weather brings. Nothing like a sweltering August afternoon to bring forth yearnings for those brisk, January, snow-crunching mornings, or vice-versa. Midwesterners actually like that variety and grow to depend on it.

The weather is a large part of what defines the peculiarity of the Midwest. We put up with a *lot*. No single factor influences our daily lives in quite the same way as weather does—what we wear, the kinds of activities we can do, the amount of time we spend indoors or out, our appetites and moods all seem to be affected by what's going on outside.

But in weather as in garage sales, one man's junk is another man's treasure. There are those for whom the forecast of rain, snow, or a mercury reading of twenty degrees is cause for great joy, while for others, the news is bad, bad, bad. The survivor types among us work and play in all kinds of weather. We've learned to be flexible in the face of its changeable elements and we've learned to appreciate the contrasts. There is nothing like that week in April or May, depending on latitude, when the corner turns from winter to spring and the smell of lilacs fills midwestern noses. The freshness, the new beginning—it's a palpable, annual thing in the Midwest. The bare branches weren't really dead after all. In a matter of days they transform themselves from gray to a hazy aura of pale-to-brighter-to-summer green. It's not that other parts of the country don't have spring, but we hear so many disparaging comments about our winters that it tends to make us a bit defensive about the glories of spring.

Meanwhile the fairly predictable annual patterns are interrupted by excesses and deprivations. Midwesterners know floods and tornadoes, blizzards and ice storms, and drought. People die and property is ruined. These phenomena can occur suddenly, but at least advanced technology offers some warning, which is more than our forebears had. Weather has always been one of life's risks in the Midwest, and tales of disaster and survival will continue to be part of midwestern lore and legend.

The tales and tidbits here ought to remind those who are hopeless Midwesterners why their character, or at least part of it, is the way it is. When the nature/nurture issue in human development comes up, I have to defend "nurture" as playing an important role.

Along with other influences, we are nurtured by the land, which literally "keeps one grounded," by the climate, which demands our attention and teaches us to adapt to its extreme nature, and to the current expression of accumulated local history. All of these things contribute to who we are as Midwesterners.

The Midwest is undeniably a place, and in light of the fact that everybody is from somewhere, the Midwest must take both credit and blame for making us who we are. We can't claim to be better, we don't have to admit to being worse, but we can't deny that we're a little different.

Where in the World?

The Midwest—not a continent, not an archipelago, not a state, nothing easily identified by a tidy natural border. Rather, the Midwest grew up from the inside, out of that most organic of materials—water. A look at a physical map reveals waterways that trace paths throughout the Midwest. Settlers traveled the water to reach the interior, and many of them settled along the water. The twelve states that now contain these vast water-webs were cited as the Midwest, perhaps for the first time, by historian Frederick Jackson Turner at a speech he gave during the Chicago World Exposition in 1893.

The Toledo Strip, a swath of land seventy-five miles long by five-to-eight miles wide along the Ohio/Michigan border, nearly inspired a civil war in 1838. Each state wanted the extra land. State militia eventually entered the fray, but Congress settled the matter by giving it to Ohio and compensating Michigan with what is called the Upper Peninsula. The decision was accepted, though not everyone was happy. Even today, residents, especially in the westernmost part of the peninsula **occasionally agitate** to join Wisconsin or to simply become a new state, Superior. Michigan is, of course, the only state in the continental U.S. with a quarter of it disconnected from the rest. (I understand that some of you Easterners may be learning this bit of Michigan trivia for the first time. As my mother would say, use it three times and it's yours.)

Michigan has more than 15,000 lakes.

The Homestead Act went into effect January 1, 1863. The first registered homestead in the U.S. was claimed by Daniel Freeman, a Union soldier, who filed his stake in Beatrice, Nebraska. You no doubt recall from your history class that the act provided for **160 acres to any man or woman** over the age of twenty-one who lived on the land for a period of five years and made certain improvements. Fees for the transaction ran about eighteen dollars. (Quit drooling.)

What you probably learned in school but may have forgotten: Beginning in 1787, what is now the eastern part of the Midwest (Michigan, Ohio, Indiana, Illinois, Wisconsin, and parts of Michigan) was labeled the Northwest Territory. The Northwest Ordinance—the laws used to govern the Northwest Territory—dictated that an area could **apply for statehood** when it had a population of 60,000. It also forbade slavery, encouraged education, and guaranteed freedom of religion to people who settled there.

Here's some postal history: In 1963, a boat on Lake Michigan was granted the U.S. Postal Service's **first floating zip code.** Now a letter addressed with 48222 will go to the J.W. Westcott II.

As Mount Rushmore was being completed, road engineers designed Highway 16A so tourists could travel from Route 36 to the monument. The engineers positioned the road's three tunnels and five spiral-like "pigtail bridges" in such a way to give approaching drivers **repeated peeks** at the monument. Pretty cool.

Western Reserve, a ten-county area in northeastern Ohio that surrounds Cleveland, Youngstown, and **Ashtabula,** was once claimed by Connecticut.

Chicago is the third largest city in the country with a population over 2,700,000.

That lump on the top of Minnesota? Yes, it was a goof, and yes it is the northernmost point in the lower forty-eight states. Called the Northwest Angle, the rectangular bulge was created by a **surveyor's error** in the 1820s and is composed of both water and land. The land section is on the northern part of the angle and—if you stay within Minnesota's borders—can be reached only by crossing Lake of the Woods. In order to get there by land, you have to go through Canada.

Wilbur Zelinsky, historian and scholar, described our area in his 1973 book, *Cultural Geography of the United States,* this way: "Everyone within and outside the Middle West **knows of its existence,** but no one seems sure where it begins or ends." Ho ho.

Of the nation's 100 **most populous cities,** 18 are in the Midwest. We have cities ranked 3, 6, 14, 18, 23, 25, 29, 30, 38, 42, 45, 58, 74, 77, 80, 82, 90, and 93. I suppose you expected their names. Sorry, we ran out of room.

The Salem Outcrop is the name for the ancient ocean floor that protrudes into central Indiana. Its high quality limestone was used to build the Empire State Building, Rockefeller Center, the Pentagon, and dozens of other buildings in the nation's capital. The rock is **filled with caves;** more than seven hundred have been explored by spelunkers and enjoyed by tourists. So there are seven hundred more locations for the claustrophobic to avoid.

More than 425 species of birds are seen in Kansas—from tiny hummingbirds to bald eagles.

State Nicknames

Why states gain the nicknames they have is often a mystery. And when the reason is not a mystery, it's still often puzzling.

ILLINOIS: *Land of Lincoln* (Does anyone need an explanation for this?)

INDIANA: *Hoosier State*
Why? No one seems to be certain. One tale has it that pioneers, when they heard a knock at the door, would respond "Who's here?" (Could we see a show of hands for folks who believe that one?) Another story talks about frontiersmen who were "iron-fisted" and would hush any room of dissent. (Husher = hoosier, get it? Hmmm.) Yet another story notes that Samuel Hoosier was a boss on a canal-building crew, who hired men from Indiana to work for him. So there's that story. Finally, if you go to enough books, you learn that *hoozer* is Cumberland dialect for the Anglo-Saxon word meaning high or hill. OK. Not so exciting, but it has the ring of practicality.

IOWA: *Hawkeye State*
Iowa was named after Chief Black Hawk at the suggestion of a newspaper writer. The Chief settled in Iowa after his release from prison in Illinois for fighting against White settlers.

KANSAS: *Squatter State, Jayhawk State*
Kansas was also called the Squatter State because of the way it was settled, and the Jayhawk State. Jayhawkers? Yes, but no one seems certain why. Some suggest that blue jay and hawk were blended, which is an easy answer but doesn't help much. The elusive "bird" received a reality boost when a 1940s textbook stated that the jayhawk was a bird that was native to Kansas. Oops. In the 1850s, Jayhawker came to stand for Free-Staters, who practiced lawlessness in their quest to have Kansas enter the union as a free state.

MICHIGAN: *Wolverine State, Water Wonderland State*
The reference to water is no mystery, but "Wolverine" is to some as likely as

By the 1950s, about 250,000,000 acres had been homesteaded.

"Humpback Whale." There are not currently and, according to some sources, there is little evidence that there were *ever* wolverines living in Michigan. It may be that French traders brought wolverine pelts into the area and traded them to shippers there. A wolverine, by the way, is the largest member of the weasel family, standing about a foot at the shoulder and weighing thirty to fifty pounds; they're powerful, fearless, and can capture and slay a deer. Sounds like a concrete block with claws. Yikes.

MINNESOTA: *Gopher State, North Star State, Bread and Butter State*
Why gophers, you're wondering. In 1859, a cartoon portraying railroad promoters as gophers in top hats captured the imagination of those who bestow nicknames, and the "Gopher State" was christened. The state is also called the North Star State because it lies farther north than any other state in the lower forty-eight, *but we've already been through that.* And it's been called the Bread and Butter State because of its high production of flour and dairy products.

MISSOURI: *Show Me State*
Named by Representative Willard Vandiver to demonstrate the simple common sense he represented on behalf of Missouri citizens.

NORTH DAKOTA: *Flickertail State*
North Dakota was named for the squirrels that live in the area. Since all squirrels flick their tails, one wonders how one species appropriated the distinction for itself.

OHIO: *Buckeye State*
The tree with the beautiful but poisonous nut.

SOUTH DAKOTA: *Sunshine State, Coyote State*
This is the term tourist promoters like to use, and Coyote State, describing one kind of state resident.

WISCONSIN: *Badger State*
For the miners who lived in the state long ago and spent so much time underground that they were nicknamed badgers.

If you're from the Midwest, you know that baby pigs should be patted.

Ah! Nebraska. Ah! Kansas

Avoka, Nebraska, August 19, 1885

Dear Son and Daughter and family one and all,

I write you this lovely morning after all night's rain and heavy thunder.
. . . I am back from the wild and jungles of Oregon. And thanks to the
beneficence of that band of ministering angels who have their bright
abodes in the far off skies for my safe deliverance back in the grandest
country on this side of the great beyond. [And I've traveled to St. Louis,
Ohio, Oregon, California, Washington, western Kansas . . .] I was never
so glad to get back in all my life. And I firmly believe that the greatest
calamity that ever befell the benighted nations of the ancient world
[was] they had no knowledge of the actual existence of Nebraska and I
firmly believe if our Pilgrim fathers would have discovered the Gulf and
sailed up the Mississippi and on up the old muddy and landed in
Nebraska, the new England states wouldn't be settled up yet. And I am
further convinced that Herodotus died the most miserable death
because in all of his travels and in all of his geographical research he
had no knowledge nor the pleasure to view the broad and fertile prairies
of Nebraska. Had such been my melancholy fate I have no doubt the
last feeble pulsation of my broken heart, the last faint exhalation of my
fleeting breath you would have heard me whispering—where is
Nebraska?

 . . . You know the United States commences at about 65 degrees
west longitude and continues to about the 125 degrees west longitude.
And if you will look on your map you will find we are so near a central

Green Bay, the oldest town in Wisconsin, is on the site of a mission founded in 1669.

part of this visible universe that the skies come down precisely at the same distance all around us, embracing alike the fragrant savannas of the sunlit south to the eternal solitudes of snow that mantles the ice-bound north that we have a heaven here of our own. . . . I am certain that if the immortal spirit of Homer could have looked down upon another heaven than that he had created by his own celestial genius, and viewed the beauties and wonderful resources and productions of the Beaver Valley of Kansas—I should say the artillery of Heaven would have fired a salute in honor of a great and glorious place as the Beaver Valley of Kansas . . .

written by George Washington Harshman
submitted by his granddaughter, Joyce Jessen
Lodgepole, Nebraska

In the 1940s, the Chicago train station saw 1,700 trains come and go—daily.

The Name Game

Town names became official by a government act, but that part of the process has often been preceded by checking with the post office to see if a name was available in a particular state.

● ● ●

Remember the adage, be careful what you ask for because you might get it? The citizens of Peculiar, Missouri, learned the hard way. When name after name submitted to their postmaster came back as "already in use by another town," they simply **left it in his hands,** telling him to pick something but "make it sort of peculiar." Their wishes were fulfilled.

It happens sometimes that a town's name is not particularly noteworthy, but a town springs up nearby whose name matches it in some way. This little exercise is the kind of backseat game you and your siblings played to pass time during long car trips on family vacations. Here are some matches my family discovered.

> **LAUREL** and HARDY, IOWA
> **REMUS** and ROMULUS, MICHIGAN
> **BISON** and BUFFALO, SOUTH DAKOTA
> Exciting stuff.

"**C**enter" is part of town names in Minnesota, South Dakota, Kansas, Missouri, Iowa, Indiana, and Nebraska. If that's not a **reminder** about what's in the middle, nothing is.

Eighty-seven percent of tornadoes travel in a northeasterly direction.

There is a rumor that there are **two Rome, Wisconsins,** one in Adams County and one in Jefferson County. I can't find either of you on my map, but if you're there, you know it. (Don't ask me about mail. I don't deliver it, I just send it.)

The Midwest is home to a variety of birds, so their being commemorated as town names is no surprise, but why, in the middle of the North American continent would there be a Gibbon, Nebraska? **Free-wandering apes** or what?

Lead, South Dakota, pronounced *leed,* was named for the vein or *lead* of gold found nearby. The mine is called the Home Stake Mine and is the **largest gold-producing mine** in the Western Hemisphere. I'll bet that's news to more than just a few of you.

Akron, Iowa, was named after Akron, Ohio, because early citizens anticipated that it would **grow as big.** Wrong. Population of Akron, Iowa, is 1,450. Ohio's Akron is 223,019.

Not to be forgotten—

GAS, KANSAS
(The when and why of this are known only to a special few.)

SEVEN HILLS, OHIO
(This is perfectly sensible, but there are two towns by that name.)

BUENA VISTA, INDIANA
(Also a perfectly nice name, but three towns have it.
I guess it says something about that Indiana landscape.)

Between 1953 and 1991, Kansas and Nebraska each had over 1,000 tornadoes.

The Landscape of Home

$\mathcal{I}$ grew up in a small town in southern Wisconsin where five generations of Bennetts lived before me. Sometimes I think of them— the tall, serious, bearded gentlemen dressed in black, frozen forever in pictures taken almost a hundred years ago.

I lived in a big gray house with my brothers and parents for seventeen years. Every day I walked to school—padding the pavement with the same children from afternoon kindergarten through high school.

Outside I was a happy, well-adjusted child. But inside I couldn't wait to leave. Secretly I plotted my escape, counted the days to graduation, and dreamed of the day I could leave that one-horse town to explore uncharted territory and see the world—to go to a place where no Bennett had been before!

After college, I moved from town to town and job to job. Finally I settled in another town nearly two thousand miles away. At last I had shed the shackles of my home town and found my true self.

Then, one hot summer night I returned to my hometown for my twentieth high school reunion. I traveled alone, flew into the closest airport, rented a car and at twilight began the hour-long drive home. It was one of those midwestern nights that punctuates the scorching days—you know the kind.

I threaded my way through the winding back roads and a joyous familiarity awakened in me. I drove up the hill and felt the car turn beneath the pressure of my hands on the steering wheel. My body moved in a familiar way as I navigated a road I had driven so many times before. I knew each curve, each hill, each vista. I recognized every

More than 84% of North Dakotans are, somehow or other, in agriculture.

farm and perfectly plowed field, and measured the time of year by the depth of the streams and the height of the corn. Images flew by, one after the other, and together they created a panorama of home. I settled into a meditation as I experienced the silence of the countryside, the glory of the Midwest. I live in California now, but I will always call the midwestern landscape home.

Julienne Bennett
Berkeley, California
(Born and raised in Monroe, Wisconsin)

And now a word from one of our own . . .

What I value about the Midwest is:

The sense of space and sky—ample room to walk, think and dream. I've even learned to appreciate the daily drama of our weather.

— SUSAN ALLEN TOTH, writer, St. Paul, Minnesota

Hail seldom falls between 5 a.m. and 10 a.m. A little feeling of security there.

Breathing Room Galore

Despite the many millions of people who live in the Midwest, there are large areas that are not populated. And among the large fields of crops, the centers of population vary from cities as large as Chicago or Cincinnati to towns of a few hundred or fewer. Whatever kind of roominess you prefer, you can find it in the Midwest.

• • •

North Dakota and South Dakota are forty-seventh and forty-eighth respectively when it comes to **people per square mile.** Their numbers are 9.03 and 9.02. (*That* is breathing room.)

Not surprisingly, South Dakota has only one city with more than 100,000 people, Sioux Falls, and **just barely.**

And more. South Dakota is fourth highest (after Idaho, Vermont, and Montana) for the percentage of people who **don't live in cities** or towns: 70.55 percent.

In the 1800s, prairie grasses in many areas were tall enough to **hide a horse.**

The average land value in Illinois is 1,416 dollars per acre, twelfth highest in the nation. It exceeds by a huge percentage the **five cents per acre** that Thomas Jefferson paid Napoleon Bonaparte for the land about two hundred years ago. Talk about inflation.

Mackinac Island, Michigan, allows bicycles and horses but no cars.

Alexis de Tocqueville traveled into America in 1830 and made notes for his famous work, *Democracy in America.* He describes his approach to Saginaw, Michigan. "Oaks of immense thickness without branches almost up to the top; gigantic pines . . . Marshy places **riotous with vegetation** . . . Our Indians leap in front of us for four hours without stopping, never hesitating about which path to take, and seeming to know the ground even in its slightest details. . . ." De Tocqueville and his companions were escorted to one of the *three* houses that made up Saginaw at the time. The city's population now is 211,946.

Michigan has **3,288 miles of shoreline,** more than any inland state in the country. The only state with more coast is Alaska.

Major midwestern rivers: Wabash, Illinois, Arkansas, Platte, Iowa, Des Moines, Red, Minnesota, Wisconsin, the Ohio—southern boundary of the eastern Midwest, the Missouri—**crossing or touching** five states, and the Mississippi, the "father of waters" that runs down the middle.

Minnesota's license plates announce "Land of 10,000 Lakes." For those who think it's a brag, the count actually comes out at 15,291, not counting those "ponds" of less than a ten-acre area. If those are included, the number hits 22,000. And at least a hundred of them are named **Mud Lake.**

In addition, Minnesota has more than 25,000 miles of streams and rivers. Laid end to end? Well now *that* would be **a very long river.** It's 240,000 miles to the moon, but we won't get into any of those comparisons.

Sand but not desert. The Sleeping Bear Dune near Traverse City, Michigan, seems to offer an **irresistible invitation** to tourists and locals. People can hardly keep from climbing it, and "skiing" down it. The western view from the top is Lake Michigan and the North and South Manitou Islands. Indian lore claims that the islands were two bear cubs who swam too far from shore; the dune is the weeping mother.

The source of the Mississippi River is in north central Minnesota at Lake Itasca.

The Apostle Islands, so named because **the discovering missionaries** believed there were twelve, actually number twenty-two. The establishment of the area as a National Lakeshore in 1970 has helped return the islands to their near pristine condition.

On a plaque near a farm in western Iowa: "Land Grant to Abraham Lincoln for services rendered in the Black Hawk War, 1832. Marked by the Denison Chapter of the Daughters of the American Revolution, 1923." Lincoln was given the land by a veteran, but he didn't turn the warrant in until he was running for U.S. President; he'd always said he couldn't afford to pay the taxes. He never farmed the land, of course. In fact, **he never saw it.**

Barbed wire changed the American farmscape, allowing ranchers to shape the territory their cattle could run in, and allowing farmers the luxury of planting crops without having their cattle or hogs **trample or eat them.** There were plenty of battles between cattlemen and farmers over the uses and locations of barbed wire fences, and there were objections from those who found it cruel to animals, but barbed wire eventually became as much a part of rural life as the straight country roads they followed.

The Eagle River in Wisconsin holds the **world record** for the number of lakes it links together in a chain—twenty-eight.

Collegeville, Indiana, experienced a record 116° F. July 14, 1936.

Old as the Hills

Prehistoric events in the Midwest left fossils and amazing geologic sights for us to investigate, enjoy, and ponder over. Ponder on.

• • •

The Black Hills were named by Dakota Indians, for whom they are sacred. From a distance, the dark green, **dense forests that cover the hills** appear black.

By the way, mountain-lovers may be interested in knowing that the Black Hills are older than the Rockies, Alps, and Himalayas. They're old and **worn down.**

The strange and multi-colored projections in the Badlands National Park in South Dakota, were formed out of **beds of lignite that burned** and left the mounds, monoliths, and ravines, whose colors improve with time. Harney Peak in the Badlands rises 7,242 feet.

Kettle Moraine State Forest in Wisconsin contains geological formations which were the **result of glacial activity** 20,000 years ago. Research into the Ice Age and its effects on the continent is carried on at Devil's Lake, near Baraboo, Wisconsin.

Much of the upper Midwest was covered by glaciers, but northeastern Iowa, southeastern Minnesota, and southwest Wisconsin along the Mississippi River **escaped the big ices.** The rougher terrain in those areas is the result of active streams.

Petrified Wood Park at Lemmon, South Dakota, displays petrified tree sections with a ten-foot diameter. Yes, ten feet! A local museum displays fossils that are **200,000,000 years old.**

One in every seven Ohioans is employed in agriculture.

The Wyandotte cave, near Curby, Indiana, is known for having what may be the **largest interior mountain**—yes, a mountain inside a cave. I know it sounds weird. My question is: Why hasn't there been an *Indiana Jones* movie here?

Cascade Falls in Minnesota drops eight stories. Minnehaha, in Minneapolis, falls fifty-three feet and was immortalized in **Henry Wadsworth Longfellow's** poem, "The Song of Hiawatha." If you're from a certain generation, you probably know that poem by heart.

During the logging era, which lasted nearly seventy years, enough trees were cut from Michigan's forests to construct **10,000,000 six-room houses.** Rather mind-boggling.

Devil's Lake, near Baraboo, Wisconsin, is spring-fed, bounded on three sides by quartzite cliffs, and has **no visible outlet.** I know it sounds like a riddle, but I have no answer.

Approximately sixty areas of **original prairie** still exist in Iowa. The largest, Hayden Prairie, is near Cresco, in the western part of the state; it's 240 acres.

Vandalia, Illinois, was the second capital of that state.

Living Off the Land

Agriculture is the life-blood of the Midwest. It's not that everyone's a farmer, but a good percentage of Midwesterners are related to farmers. And an even larger percentage raise vegetables. Midwesterners are fanatical gardeners, which is dandy for those few who aren't. I doubt there's an employee staff room anywhere in the Midwest that doesn't have a box on the table in August with a hand-lettered invitation, "free tomatoes" or, the gods help us, "free zucchini."

● ● ●

Agriculture was the reason that in 1959, the Premier of the Union of Soviet Socialist Republics, Nikita Khrushchev, paid a visit to Iowa. He wanted to see a typical farm and was taken to Roswell Garst's place near Coon Rapids. Garst was a successful farmer with a seed corn business. **He and Nikita got along famously**. Garst reported that the two of them "laughed and yelled back and forth" for a few hours.

Minnesota is **tops in the nation** in sugar beets, second in hay and dairy products, and third in oats.

As of 1947, one-fourth of the nation's **first-class farm land,** as designated by the U.S. Department of Agriculture, was in Iowa.

Are you ready for some incredible numbers? U.S. farms decreased by 44,000 between 1990 and 1992; six thousand of them were in Ohio. The state is tenth nationally in number of farms. The farms, of course, didn't fall into **a black hole;** they were sold to neighbors or corporations. Perhaps it should be read that *farmers* decreased by 44,000. (Don't quote me; I'm just doing a little speculating.)

Collegeville, Minnesota, had 66.4 inches of snow in March 1965.

Well, gee, that midwestern pride. The story is told of a farmer who was riding a train from St. Louis back home to Indiana. He was bragging about the size, hardiness, and success of everything in his state. When he finished **a glowing comparison of grasshoppers** to his jumbo thumb, he proclaimed with a grin, "It shows how productive the land is."

An unwelcome invasion into the Dakotas in the 1870s was the tumbleweed. It was known as Russian cactus, **wind witch, and Russian thistle.** The Russian connection had to do with settlers believing that immigrants had imported it, since it reportedly resembled a plant common in Odessa in southern Russia.

The tumbleweed's sharp, spiny leaves could cut the skin of ranchers and animals alike. Farmers avoided working with bundles of grain overrun with it, but horses might run through infested pastures, harming themselves severely, before farmers realized what had happened. When horses were disabled, the entire homestead was threatened. To make matters worse, the tumbleweed's mobility, literally bouncing across the land, meant that it could carry fire far and wide, too. It's not surprising to learn that some people abandoned their homes and fields because of the pernicious weed.

Aren't you amazed to learn that **Ohio is first** in the production of African violets?

Henry A. Wallace, Iowan, who served as Secretary of Agriculture and then vice-president under President Franklin D. Roosevelt, helped encourage New Deal **practices that affected farmers,** including soil conservation, standardization of produce prices, and price supports. A useful bit of farming history for you.

Kansas. Its grand sweeping fields of wheat that are often compared to "oceans," so you may be **breathless with astonishment** to learn that the state is also home to 55,000 ponds and watersheds. Fishing—not just farming—is big business.

There are about 100,000 buffalo now in the U.S.

Words to eat: ". . . not one acre in a hundred that would in any case **admit of cultivation** . . ." So said early land surveyor Edward Tiffin about Michigan.

Silage is livestock feed that is made from corn, including the stalk. The plant is ground up when there is still moisture in it, and the plant ensiles. Ensiles? Stored without oxygen (in silos, of course), the **pulverized plant** undergoes an organic activity that resembles fermentation. Now you know more about that contented look on the faces of cows. About ten percent of the U.S. corn crop is used for silage.

In 1993, a flathead catfish weighing ninety pounds was caught in the Pamona Reservoir in Kansas (Osage County). Fishery biologists estimate that **fish weighing up to a hundred pounds** live in Kansas waters.

Norman E. Borlaug, an agronomist who developed **new varieties of wheat,** was born in 1914 in Cresco, Iowa. In 1970, he was awarded the Nobel Peace Prize for his food production innovations.

Michigan has about 4,000 oil-producing wells.

Weather or Not

Weather plays a big part in defining the rhythm of midwestern life. It has the power to cause a drastic rearrangement in human plans—an outside wedding moves in, a cook-out becomes a cook-in—but the rhythm it causes is (almost) pure pleasure to a lot of Midwesterners. A change of wardrobe means stashing the sweaters for a few months, and later it means boxing up those shorts. Eating customs shift from outdoor grilling, picnics, and local produce to slow-cookers and frozen or imported vegetables. Fireplaces are cleaned and woodpiles rise and fall. From the echoing natatorium to outdoor pools in the sunshine and wind. Some people are elated when the first snow hits, and others can't wait for the swelter of July. We're forced to accept change.

The weather prevents us from having all the things we like available to us all the time. It forces us to follow cycles—we can have this, we can't have this, we can do this, we can't do this. And it contributes to the delight of getting what we want when the time is right. If anticipation offers any innate pleasures—and some say it's the best pleasure—Midwesterners might have the most joyous lives possible. Delayed gratification is built into our sensibility. And it may not be an altogether bad thing.

• • •

The **largest hailstone on record** fell on Coffeyville, Kansas, in September 1970. It weighed over one-and-a-half pounds and measured more than seventeen inches around. Stones of nearly the same size fell near Potter, Nebraska, in 1928 and in Dubuque, Iowa, in 1882. I'll bet there were some sleepless nights for insurance agents.

Only about 20% of lightning activity occurs between the clouds and the ground.

Thunderstorms are most likely in late afternoon and early evening. **But you knew that.**

Earthquakes are usually thought of as a West Coast phenomenon despite the fact that New Madrid, Missouri, in 1911 and 1912 experienced three of them—all stronger than the famous 1906 earthquake that destroyed San Francisco. **Rumor has it** that the New Madrid quakes caused bells to ring in Washington, D.C.

Author **Patricia Hampl** recalls, "We took pride in our wretched weather ('St. Paul-Minneapolis is the coldest metropolitan area *in the world*,' my mother read to us from the paper) the way a small nation does its national art, as if the ice cube, our symbol, were the supreme artifact of civilization."

Summer in the Midwest means driving down gravel roads, where the dust rises in a **lazy whirl** before slowly easing back down to the ground.

Cold Friday of 1807 (not to be confused with New England's Cold Friday of 1810) was a day when a cold chill pushed down from the Great Lakes, bringing in a rain storm that turned to snow. **And it raged.** The temperature dropped a giant fifty-nine degrees, falling to minus eleven.

In western South Dakota, a bad year might bring a **mere seven inches** of rain. A good year, fifteen. Compare that with Chicago's thirty-three, or New York's forty-four.

Zap, North Dakota—one of the shortest city names in the Midwest.

During the Big Snow of 1967 in Chicago, Illinois, among the passengers waylaid at O'Hare Airport were **the Rolling Stones.** (This was previously a little-known fact, and I'm not divulging how I know it.)

A clear night in June in the Midwest is perfect for star gazing: The North Star, the Little and Big Dippers, **the Pleiades are all twinkling.** And when your neck is tired, the darkened lawns are the perfect backdrop for the strange flicker of fireflies.

The year 1975 brought to Minnesota one of its "Storms of the Century." The wind chill temperature was minus fifty to minus eighty degrees. Snow measured twenty-three and one-half inches in some places, and there were **thirty-five storm-related deaths.**

Warren, Ohio, suffered **excessive and unseasonal snowfall** in late April 1901 with a twenty-eight-inch accumulation. Twenty-eight inches!

In March 1966, Minnesota and North Dakota suffered a blizzard with winds up to **one hundred miles per hour** for more than one hundred hours. It might build our character, but it doesn't mean we think it's fun.

Even though it's a short month, February 1958, holds the record for **snowfall in Indiana.** The town was LaPorte, and the amount was 59.8 inches.

Kansas City, Missouri, had a **flash flood** in September 1977, after repeated downpours in one thirty-six-hour period. From twelve to sixteen inches of rain fell in the area. Tragically, seventeen people died in their cars, eight others died in flood-related circumstances.

The average life of a tornado on the ground is less than 15 minutes.

Spring Thaw

Our farm was one short mile from the small, southwest Iowa town of Massena, down a dirt road that included one of those big hills straight out of a Grant Wood painting.

My parents were devout Catholics, and we went into Massena to church every Sunday morning regardless of the condition of the road. Many a spring morning, I remember that monster hill being frozen solid as we tooled into town in our Sunday best, but before the final blessing it would thaw enough that Dad's old Model A couldn't make it up the hill.

The car would struggle about a quarter of the way on the first try. With Mom and the latest baby in the front and the rest of us packed into the back, Dad would back the car down for another run at it. Dad would push the gas pedal to the floor, and we'd fly at the hill. We probably topped out at about thirty miles an hour. Most of the time, several runs would get us about halfway up, and that was it.

Shoes were expensive and it was out of the question for us to risk ruining them in the mud, so we'd slip them off, roll pant legs or hoist skirts, and walk home. Sometimes Mom and we girls would not only remove our shoes and stockings, but our clean, starched dresses to protect them from mud splatters, and we would walk to the house in our slips.

I can still see Dad leading the way up that hill with his shoes slung over his shoulders, his pant legs rolled knee-high, and the baby in his arms. Later, he'd hitch up the team and pull the car home.

Norma Henkenius Schaaf
Massena, Iowa

State Center, Iowa, by the way, isn't.

Wild About Tornadoes

Tornado tales are part of midwestern lore. The behavior of these awe-inspiring twisters, their destructive power, and the baffling phenomena they often leave in their wake are the stuff of many a narrative. Everyone has a story to tell, either one of their own or something they've heard. Me, too. I knew people in Fargo, North Dakota, whose home was severely damaged by a tornado in the 1950s. When the family emerged from the basement, a roll of paper towels still rested on the top of the refrigerator; the watch that had lain next to it was gone. In their dining room, they found a small vase with fresh flowers and water that had been sitting in the center of the table; the vase was still upright with flowers and water, but now it sat on the underside of the table, which had been flipped during the cyclone.

● ● ●

Tornadoes are classified according to their power. Categories include "Doubtful," for one that merely breaks off twigs, to "Very Weak," "Weak," which could break windows and push moving cars off roads, "Strong," "Severe," "Devastating," where frame houses are turned into rubble and cars are lifted or rolled a good distance, to "Incredible" which completely debarks trees and performs *incredible* phenomena. You've seen pictures of a **check sliced halfway through a telephone pole?** And last are the "Inconceivable" tornadoes, which throw large car-sized objects for long distances. Such a tornado is, well, inconceivable.

May is **the most likely month for tornadoes,** but they can happen any time. They also rarely occur between 3:00 A.M. and 5:00 A.M. In the Midwest, they generally come on during late afternoon and early evening.

Michigan has 120,000 miles of roads.

In a survey of over 18,000 tornadoes, it was determined that the average width of the path is about 140 yards. Few of them are over seven hundred yards, but it is not uncommon for the very large ones to spread their energy across several miles as they swirl toward their collapse. And I don't have to tell you how many football fields fit into seven hundred yards. That's wide. And 140 is **nothing to sneeze at** either.

In modern times, the longest known track of a tornado was 293 miles. The twister spent 188 miles in Illinois, during the beginning of which there was **possibly a little skipping,** and 105 miles in Indiana. It occurred in May of 1917. Amazing.

The **greatest outbreak of tornadoes** in the nation's history occurred in 1974, in the early hours of April 4. The first one appeared in northern Illinois. And then 147(!) more appeared in the same storm system. The affected area stretched from Detroit, Michigan, to Atlanta, Georgia, from central Illinois to east of Roanoke, Virginia; 315 people were killed.

The most destructive single tornado on record traveled 219 miles from Redford, Missouri, to Princeton, Indiana. The event took place March 18, 1925, and **killed 695 people,** injured 2,027 and caused property damage estimated at 17,000,000 dollars. That's depressing. Makes us grateful for Doppler radar and our favorite weather men and women.

How fast do tornado winds blow? No one knows for sure. What *is* known for sure is that **winds of 125 miles per hour can cause damage,** and winds of two hundred miles per hour can cause severe damage. Along with great speeds go great drops in barometric pressure—the greatest that occur on the surface of the earth. And as I write this, there is a tornado watch a few miles up the road. Can you beat that?

Wisconsin's Fox River flows north.

Forbears Toughing It Out

or

... THE ICE ON THE RIVER IS THICKER THAN HITHERTO ...

In the winter of 1804–05, Lewis and Clark camped by the Missouri River near several tribal villages, close to the present site of Bismarck, North Dakota. Their daily reports included thermometer notes and other descriptions. They are, however, notably free of whining, complaint, or anger at the fates. Frankly, it's a bit humbling. Here are a few:

November 17, 1804. Last night was very cold, and the ice in the river is thicker than hitherto. The frost of yesterday remained on the trees until 2 P.M. when it descended like a shower or snow; swans passing from the north.

December 16. The morning is clear and cold, the mercury at sunrise 22 degrees below zero.

December 20. . . . the thermometer 24 above 0 at sunrise.

January 10, 1805. [With the morning reading at forty below, Clark reports that some Indians were caught in the snow over night, one with no fire, and yet came in without frost. Another spent the night in moccasins, leggings and a buffalo robe. His feet were frozen and the white men put them in cold water and gave him] every attention in our power. [He added that the] Indians support the rigors of the season in a way which we had hitherto thought impossible.

March 5. 40 degrees. [The following day he reports cloudiness and] smoky in consequence of the burning of the plains by the Minnetarees; they have set all the neighboring country on fire in order to obtain an early crop of grass which may answer for the consumption of their horses. The river rose a little and overran the ice, so as to rend the crossing difficult.

Illinois' leading agricultural products are corn, soybeans, hogs, and cattle.

Odd Facts

Cleveland, Ohio, was the first American city to have electric street lights. The year was 1879. **People thought they'd go blind** and closed their eyes.

Cloud County, Kansas, on a hill south of Concordia, was the site in September 1876 of a snake-killing that lasted over four weeks and left **more than four thousand snakes** dead. Yuck.

It's probably an old story that map makers can cause wars, but it happened not so long ago in Wisconsin. The year was 1967 and the place was Winneconne, a town of two thousand that was omitted from the new state map. The residents were upset, and they invited people to offer suggestions about what they might do. Two Wisconsin girls living in Washington, D.C., offered the winning solution: **secede and declare war.** Indeed, the action is a time-honored way to get some attention, and it worked. Winneconne declared its secession on July 22 with the Winneconne Navy, Air Force, and Army on hand for the event. They issued a Declaration of Independence and set up a toll bridge over the Wolf River to raise state revenue. By the end of the day, they had collected seven dollars. Negotiations, of course, began immediately, and by noon the next day, they were once again part of the state. Is it any coincidence that Wisconsin now has a law making it illegal to declare war against the state?

John Muir was born in Scotland and died in California, but his route from one place to the other was not direct. He spent his boyhood, which he recounted in detail in *The Story of My Boyhood and Youth,* in Columbia County, Wisconsin. The countryside instilled in him his lifelong interest in nature. But he also had

Iowa has 112,000 miles of paved roads and highways.

a love for innovation, and he **invented clocks madly**—one tipped him out of bed in the morning, and another cleverly ignited the fire at the rural school where he taught, an hour before classes began.

Griggsville, Illinois, is the Purple Martin Capital of the World, but the town didn't gain such a distinction without working at it. It all began with a terrible **mosquito problem,** and since purple martins are such avid mosquito-eaters, the townspeople followed that *Field of Dreams* advice: "If you build it, they will come." In this case, what they built were 504 nesting locations for the birds. They came, they ate, they stayed.

An elephant named Norma Jean, who weighed in at 6,500 pounds, met a sad end in July of 1974 in Oquawka, Illinois, when the tree she was chained to was struck by lightning.

It was once a common practice for towns to close a steep street during the winter and **reserve it for sledders.** The custom has largely faded as cars have become so prevalent, but it still is practiced in some places, including Mount Vernon, Iowa.

Hogs have a reputation for being rowdy and malicious when they root up the pastures, but in fact they're looking to satisfy their hearty appetites and that **ongoing urge** for, well, for roots. (Remember, to a pig, the underground delicacy called a truffle is just another snack.)

A road in Burlington, Iowa, is said by Ripley's *Believe It or Not,* to be the **least straight road** in the world. Aptly called Snake Alley, the road has five half-curves and two quarter-curves within about one-nineteenth of a mile or 275 feet. Sounds like the flat version of a roller coaster.

October 8, 1871. A forest fire raged through Peshtigo, Wisconsin; it was **the very night** of the Great Chicago Fire. In the well-known fire, 250 people died; in the forgotten fire, one thousand people died. Go figure.

Kalamazoo, Michigan, had a tough time in its early days. Residents tried to promote a new cash crop—celery. **Citizens were skeptical** of its safety (it resembles hemlock) until one grower sent his children door-to-door to sell it.

Ann Ellsworth of Lafayette, Indiana, was invited by Samuel F.B. Morse to offer the first words sent across the wire in the original inter-city telegraph exchange, **between Baltimore and Washington, D.C.** She chose "What hath God wrought?" And advances and controversy in telecommunications since that May 24, 1844, event have inspired the same thought again and again.

Single farmers across the Midwest have begun **to organize to find wives.** The flurry even inspired a story in *The New York Times* in 1995. One such group is in Herman, Minnesota. I wonder if some action on "The Dating Game" would help.

It was the summer of 1893 when Anton Dvořák came to Spillville, Iowa, to live and work. He polished parts of the "New World Symphony" and wrote a quartet during his stay. His **strolls along Turkey River** and through the woods reportedly inspired "Humoresque." The house he stayed in is now partly used as the Bily Clocks Museum of unique and sometimes gargantuan hand-carved clocks. And the organ that he played weekly at St. Wenceslaus Church is being restored, if supporters can raise the funds.

The average age of midwestern farmers is 52.

Field Treasures

Somewhere between an old farm house and a cemetery sprawls a bumpy, torn field. It is fairly small—driving by it takes less than a minute. The field stands remarkably empty of structures other than a few rusty, short poles and a small trailer bed. I pass this way just about every day on my way to work, barely noticing it.

Yet, when company comes—my aunt and cousin from near Los Angeles, California, or my father, who lives dead center in the throbbing heart of Chicago, we go to the field. We drive past the field, slowly, as slow as possible, and my passengers strain to gaze onto the tufted field just alongside the road.

"Look! There's one! And another! Look over there! See his little head pop out! What's he eating—is he eating something?! Look, one is running across to another hole!"

My family is fascinated by this display of the busy community activity from, of all things, ground squirrels or prairie dogs, hundreds of them in their village, out in the open, in nature, not cooped up in the simulated pseudo-natural environment of a zoo, but as free as possible.

For my "citified" family, the sight is indeed a rare treat. I stare at the field hoping no young entrepreneur has any development designs on this piece of forgotten land. Gripping my steering wheel, I contentedly smile as I realize that the mere existence of "forgotten land" in our overcrowded world is one of the things that makes living in the Midwest such an irreplaceable, magical thing!

Lynn Ledeboer
Hutchinson, Kansas

Indiana has about 90,000 miles of roads.

What's in a Name?

*Names, in a family or in a place, often track a history of what was impor-
tant, cultural interests, or a special occurrence. Lighter moments have
ruled many names, too.*

• • •

Despite **its exotic look**, Cairo, Illinois, is pronounced like Karo, the syrup.

And then there's **MADrid, Iowa,** and Russia [ROOshe], Ohio. I don't know
why these things happen.

Indiana has some charming names for towns and geographical features. For
instance—Rural and Farmers, Bruce Lake and Lake Bruce, Tulip and Dog-
wood, and **Old Bath and New Bath.** These last two may suggest something
about water availability.

Scipio and Scipio, Indiana. One is named for a Roman General and one is
named for a Peoria Chief, and one of them is partly in Ohio. Only one has the
postmaster general's blessing; you'll have to find out which one. (I'm only
the author here; I'm not your mom.)

Vincennes, Indiana, is **the state's oldest town,** founded possibly as a French
trading post about 1683 and serving as the capital of the Northwest Territory.
Old, old.

The following list is, yes, names of towns in our own Midwest:
>   Wahoo and **Suprise** in Nebraska (Yes, it's Suprise without the "r."
>   Don't harrass them.)
>   What Cheer and **Gravity** in Iowa
>   **Zap** and Cando in North Dakota

At the very center of Ohio is a town called Delaware.

Wee Soil and **Hell** in Michigan
Novelty and **Utopia** in Ohio
Chicken Bristle and Normal in Illinois
Imalone in Wisconsin
Pure Air and **Tightwad** in Missouri

Choose your body part. We have to wonder a bit how towns gained names from body parts. Your guess is as good as mine.

Sleepy Eye, Minnesota
Elbow Lake, Minnesota
Colon, Nebraska
Palms, Michigan
Rib Lake, Wisconsin
Fortunately, **Monkeys Eyebrow** is across the Ohio River in Kentucky.

Some **place names give you a surprise** because things aren't where you thought they were. Thoroughly confused? Try this. New England, North Dakota, or, how about Virginia, Minnesota? Confused enough? There's Lisbon, Iowa; Dearborn, Missouri; El Paso, Illinois; and Galveston, Indiana. Enough? Take two aspirin and call me in the morning.

And here are some mood names. Do you suppose **life is somehow a little different** for citizens of these towns?

Paradise, Kansas
Luck, Wisconsin
Justice, Illinois
Bravo, Michigan
Brilliant, Ohio
Paragon, Indiana *and*
Chagrin Falls, Ohio

More than 90% of North Dakota is farm land.

Our Work Ethic

*To work—to work! It is such infinite delight to know
that we still have the best things to do.*

– Katherine Mansfield (1888–1923)

The midwestern work ethic dates back to the first settlers and the circumstances of their lives. Pioneers had no choice but to do for themselves: If they didn't take care of things, nothing happened. Their predicament was not unlike that of the first colonizers on the continent two hundred years earlier. But it is remarkable that while many were leaving lives of privation and little hope, others left lovely homes with glass windows and well-stocked nearby stores, sacrificing much of what they had in order to risk starting over in the hope it would lead to an even better life. Their few possessions—whatever fit into a covered wagon or, later, a few trunks on the train—inevitably meant that they had to take responsibility for invention of all kinds at all levels, beginning with capturing or digging for food and slicing slabs of sod to build homes on the prairie.

Men, women, and children devoted most of their waking hours to the improvement of their homes and their land, taking care of animals or each other, and planning in whatever ways they could for the coming season. The more help the better, so it was an era when large families were common. A woman often bore ten children or more. And she also wove fabric to sew into clothing, tended to the garden and the chickens, too, plus cooking and housework. The men worked in the fields and took care of the large animals and whatever equipment they had to help them with their work.

Leisure wasn't a part of life the way it is now, but people made time to read, to beautify their homesteads, to attend events at school or church, and to celebrate with feasting after large tasks, such as barn-raisings.

People worked, and they worked hard. They toiled on the farm—watching their crops or herds or homesteads grow, inventing better ways to plant or plow—or in the cities, starting businesses, working for others, developing better ways to process or transport goods, or to prepare and package foods. The decades surrounding the settlement of the Midwest seem marked by a spirit of determination and a mood of accomplishment. The energy generated by an abundance of opportunity and the prospect of success made work an integral part of the American dream: Hard work leads to a better life.

It's no surprise that the can-do attitude still prevails in the Midwest. The legacy is strong, and it's a relatively recent phenomenon—one or two generations back for many of us. We still carry the tales of good fortune from our ancestors—those who had the tools, the skills, and the boldness to take on the challenge, also had the prime midwestern gift of bounteous natural resources. And that plenitude no doubt contributed to the creativity and innovation that were so often part of daily life, a part of the adapting to and making do. Problems were seen as puzzles to solve rather than as conditions to live with. The solutions that Midwesterners developed often led to sustainable small businesses or, occasionally, to giant corporations that have had and continue to have a huge impact on our lives.

Although Americans all across the country were developing new or better ways to do virtually everything, the word "innovator" was in fact seen for a time as synonymous with "Midwesterner"—probably because so much was happening in the Midwest, in terms of agricultural, industrial, and domestic improvements.

But it's not only the can-do attitude and proclivity for innovation that have endured: Two other aspects of the work ethic have flourished. One is the usefulness of working together on larger projects. Farm cooperatives still exist, and their obvious progeny, food co-ops that began in the late 1960s and early 1970s, are still bustling enterprises in many midwestern communities. The other legacy from the era of settlement is the independent spirit that drives people to press forth on their own, so the Midwest boasts a lot of solo stars, too, fiercely determined to be, to do, to accomplish in their chosen field.

Volumes could be written to chronicle the pioneer spirit and the multitude of good midwestern ideas that have led to successes of all kinds and to improved lives for Americans. Every town, every family, every city block has its story. What follows is a small sampling of some of the work and enterprises indigenous to the Midwest.

Wash Days, 1918-21

We lived on the homestead at Birchdale, Minnesota, where Saturday—wash day—was quite an event. During the snowy months of winter, when our shallow well was rock hard, we kept a fifty-gallon wood-stave vinegar barrel next to the old wood-burning cook stove. We kept the barrel full of clean snow that melted down to soft water. I think my brother and I figured it took ninety-seven pails of snow to make one half-barrel of water. This was enough for the wash water and baths.

The fleece-lined union suits were hung outside with the arms hung over the line. They froze solid and we brought them in and stood them around the stove, where they looked like ghosts. As they thawed, they were picked up and hung over chairs. The other clothes were hung on lines or racks inside.

During the rainy season of summer, the barrel was placed under the homemade wood eaves to catch the rain water. In the early fall when we went out to fill the wash basin, we often had to break a crust of ice.

The dry spells of summer were the fun times. Families would call each other during the week and make plans for a big wash day at Reverend Howard's river bank on Rainy River. Food and laundry were loaded on wagons and buggies, and we all headed for the river. It was a perfect place, with a long grassy slope where the washed clothes could be spread out to dry. The men kindled fires and placed logs or rocks around them to balance the wash tub and boilers. The white clothes were boiled, yes, boiled.

Wisconsin became the first state to identify highways by numbers.

We children had the time of our lives, trying to catch fish, wading in the water, chucking rocks and sticks in the river and tearing around like all kids do. The men and big boys were busy with getting wood for the fires, passing around a bottle or two of home brew, and catching fish for the big outdoor meal.

How the time flew by, but we always looked forward to another wash day at the river.

Albert E. Johnson
International Falls, Minnesota

Fuel Gathering

I grew up in the sandhills of Cherry County, Nebraska. We had a heating stove in the living room and a cook stove in the kitchen. There were no trees for firewood to burn, so we three boys would hitch up a team and wagon every Saturday in the fall and go to the cattle pasture to pick up dried cow chips for stove fuel. We would fill a large shed and stack a huge pile outside also. We carried in about three old wash tubs of chips every evening so Mom would have enough to last through the next day until we got home from school to carry in more. They made good heat but created a lot of dust and a lot of ashes to carry out. We did this for many winters, until kerosene stoves came on the scene.

Charles R. Giles
Broken Bow, Nebraska

At the Sloan Museum in Flint, Michigan you can see a 10,000-year-old mastodon skeleton.

The Inventive Spirit

Settlers, who arrived in the Midwest with a mere covered wagon full of goods, expected to use available resources to create the things they needed from the resources they could find. That custom fed an energy and a conviction that became a legacy passed on to the next generation. For many of us, this propensity for invention began only a generation or two ago.

• • •

Bell Aircraft Corporation, developers of commercial helicopters and the plane that Chuck Yaeger flew when he **broke the sound barrier,** was founded by Lawrence Bell, Mentone, Indiana. (Mentone—also a town with a large egg. See p. 142)

The American Beauty Rose was developed at Hill Floral Products in Richmond, Indiana. The company, begun by E. Gurney Hill in 1905, now has forty acres of greenhouses and ships **20,000,000 roses** yearly all over the Midwest and South. Twenty million, and I know maybe two people who got them. Where are all these lucky recipients?

Billy Scholl was one of thirteen children raised on a dairy farm in LaPorte County, Indiana. His early interest and skill as the family's unofficial shoe repairman inspired his parents to send him to apprentice with a local cobbler. From there Billy went to Chicago where the conditions of his customers' feet

Dexter, Iowa, was named for a horse.

made him decide to enter **Illinois Medical College.** His aids have made Americans much more foot conscious, not to mention grateful for that array of blue and orange packaging that signals relief is on the way.

Abraham Lincoln, who is rightfully claimed by several midwestern states (he lived in two of them and spent time in others), tried his hand at inventing and developed a way to **help boats ride over shallows.** His contraption involved cylinders that could be inflated. He was granted a patent in 1849, but his political career was taking off, and he had no time to promote the idea with the shipping industry.

George Safford Parker was a teacher in Janesville, Wisconsin. He was unhappy with the quality of his students' writing instruments. The solution? Invent a better pen. In 1889, he received a patent for his fountain pen. He and partner, W.F.Palmer, built a thriving business. The fountain pen became **a status symbol**—those who had one could obviously, or seemingly, read and write. The company introduced the world's first ball point pen in 1956. Quick, what was it called? Answer: the Jotter.

Fort Howard, makers of Green Forest tissue and paper towels and owner of Ecosource, which recycles over a million tons of wastepaper annually, neither owns nor leases any forested land. The company also is **self-sufficient,** making its own electricity and many of the chemicals it needs for manufacturing. Austin Cofrin began the company in 1919. Located in Green Bay, Wisconsin, it's the largest manufacturer of tissue products in the country.

Garrett Morgan, famous Black inventor and businessman from Ohio, developed an **automatic traffic signal** in 1923.

Tribune, Kansas, was named for Horace Greeley's paper.

Thomas Alva Edison is one of Ohio's most favorite sons, born there in 1847 in Milan. At age seventeen, he built a telegraph set, and later he invented what would eventually be the record player, and more and more wonderful devices, not the least of which was the **world-transforming light bulb**. The incandescent wonder appeared in 1879.

Laurens Hammond, Evanston, Illinois, invented the electric clock and then developed an "electronic keyboard" that he called an organ. Smitten with the possibilities of electricity, he also developed the now-forgotten card table that electrically shuffled and **dealt a hand of bridge.** There must be some interesting reasons why Las Vegas has never pursued such an apparatus.

The first matchbook was manufactured in **Barberton, Ohio,** in 1896 by the Diamond Match Company.

The pinball game was invented by Chicago, Illinois' In and Outdoor Games Company in 1930. The first one was called **The Whoopee Game** and was based on a children's game, Bagatelle. It measured twenty-four by forty-eight inches and for a nickel, players got ten balls. Does anyone recall why pinball was seen as such a sin? (Besides the fact that they were often in smoky bars.)

Indiana truck drivers Don Kenworthy and Conrad Gentry were the first to seek permission to **transport people's belongings** beyond state lines—in fact, all over the nation. They were also the first to train their employees in how to pack up households. Their business began in 1917, and they called it Mayflower Transit.

Percentage of days of possible sunshine on a yearly basis in Cincinnati, Ohio—52%.

The wife of Elwood Haynes, of early car history, told her husband that she wished she had silverware that wouldn't tarnish. Elwood, with a fervor that exemplifies what **an eager spouse** can do, took action and invented stainless steel. Wow.

Once again, necessity shows itself to be the mother of invention. Almon Strowger, a Kansas City, Kansas, undertaker, was losing business. When people rang for his services, the operator would connect the calls to **a rival undertaker**—her husband. Strowger invented a telephone system that didn't need a human go-between. For reasons I do not know, however, the first such system was installed in LaPorte, Indiana, in 1892. Do you suppose people in Indiana were also quicker to go for caller ID, call waiting, and other technological wizardries?

The suction vacuum cleaner was invented by Chicago, Illinoisan Ives McGaffrey. The Hoover Company in North Canton, Ohio, was **the first manufacturer of vacuum cleaners.** And aren't we all glad about that.

The zipper was invented by Chicagoan Whitcomb Judson in 1893. He later sold his Chicago, Illinois, company, **the Universal Fastener Company,** to Goodrich, who installed zippers in their rubber boots.

George Washington Gale Ferris of Galesburg, Illinois, gave us **the fabulous ferris wheel,** which seems so common to us now that we don't even capitalize the F.

Lincoln Logs were developed by Frank's son, **John Lloyd Wright,** who spent much of his young life in southwest Wisconsin. He began marketing them in 1916. Today Lincoln Logs are owned by Playskool, and the logs are made in Washington state from pine trees.

Mellen, Wisconsin, had 11.72 inches of rain in one day—June 24, 1946.

A returning fad that refuses to fade is the **Lava Lite,** manufactured by Lava Simplex Internationale in Chicago. The machine entertains viewers by generating bubbles that slowly rise through a thick, colored liquid, based on a secret recipe of eleven chemicals. So much for the hours and hours of party-time spent puzzling over some theories of mixing oil and water.

Barbed wire was invented in DeKalb, Illinois, either by Joseph F. Glidden or by Jacob Haish; the dispute led to long, drawn-out, patent-infringement cases. Regardless of which story you believe, the claim was settled legally February 29, 1892, by the U.S. Supreme Court when it granted the patent to Joseph F. Glidden. But **both men made money,** and DeKalb benefitted by gaining two hospitals, one bearing the name of Glidden and the other, Haish.

A Wisconsin business that changed direction from its original goal was begun by Samuel Johnson. Initially, he sold parquet flooring, but he eventually focused on products designed to care for wood floors. Having visited **European castles** where he learned that they used wax on their floors, he studied Carnauba wax and introduced it into his line of products. The rest, as they say, is history. The S.C. Johnson headquarters are in Racine in a landmark Frank Lloyd Wright building, triangular with rounded corners, that opened in 1939.

Cellophane tape was invented by Richard G. Drew of St. Paul, Minnesota, in 1928 and marketed by 3M (Minnesota Mining and Manufacturing). The same patent granted to Drew in 1928 for cellophane tape included masking tape. Who would have imagined that stickiness could have so many uses?

Free **home delivery of mail** was conceived by Joseph W. Briggs of Cleveland, Ohio, in 1863. Bless him.

Nearly 5% of Ohio's farms are managed by women.

Illinois' Elgin watches were the **Rolls Royce of timepieces,** with a price tag of 117 dollars each in 1867. The cost fell as production methods became streamlined, but the watches were always known for being accurate, long-lasting, and classy.

Newton, Iowa, is home of Maytag, which for a long time has been associated almost exclusively with clothes washing machines. It's little wonder since it was Fred Maytag who invented a gas-powered machine that would wash and wring out clothes in 1884. He began marketing the washing machine in 1907, and Newton became **the washing machine capital of the world**. (What do washing machines and cheese viruses have in common? You'll read about it elsewhere.)

Zenith Radio Corporation of Chicago, Illinois, made the first portable radio in 1924. From there the list of firsts goes on and on: black-and-white TV, color TV, remote control device, and **who knows what's next?**

Kleenex was created by Kimberly Clark in Wisconsin to remove women's make-up and was advertised that way. A letter from a creative Kleenex user, informing them that the product was also a handy handkerchief, changed things. A market survey revealed that sixty percent of the users had already discovered this alternative usage. When **the advertising focus shifted,** sales doubled. Another major product of the company, Kotex, was developed from cellulose cotton, which was a medical staple during World War II. Skeptical store owners thought women would be too self-conscious to buy the product, but wrong. Smartness outweighs embarrassment.

Verona, Wisconsin, had hailstones weighing more than one pound each on May 23, 1878.

Where Healing Happens

AN INTENSE INTEREST in learning more about how to fix the body and a desire and willingness to practice that knowledge led a doctor and his two sons from their work in refining surgical experimentation to the development of a world-renowned clinic. The roots of the Mayo Clinic lay in the medical practice of Dr. William W. Mayo, whose ancestors had practiced medicine, such as it was, in Lancashire, England, in the sixteenth century.

In addition to practicing medicine, which was not particularly lucrative, Mayo edited a newspaper, captained a steamboat, surveyed, and tried farming. His wife, Louise Abigail Wright, assisted in the family income with her sometime millinery business. She also bore six children, including two who died as babies and two sons who followed in their father's medical footsteps.

Medicine, at the close of the nineteenth century was moving into a new era, as anesthesia, antiseptic, and finally aseptic surgical procedures were introduced. The Drs. Mayo embraced the methods, and while they didn't "invent" surgical procedures, they performed them in such numbers that they were able to refine techniques, and operations became routine. They performed ten gall bladder procedures in 1895 and ten years later—324. That year, 1905, the brothers performed over two thousand abdominal surgeries. When they reported their vast numbers of operations at Eastern medical meetings, their reports were met with skepticism. But the skeptics were invited to come and observe; they did and they went away believers.

In addition to medical advances, a natural disaster ended up assisting the growth of the Mayo Clinic. A tornado destroyed a large

Gladys Pyle was the first woman elected to the U.S. Senate from South Dakota.

portion of Rochester in 1883, which helped the town realize its need for a hospital. The Sisters of St. Francis raised funds and constructed a forty-five-bed hospital in 1889. The Mayos initially comprised the hospital staff; eventually partners were added. In the years since, the hospital has grown to nearly a thousand-bed facility, and the self-perpetuating Mayo Clinic continues to supply the staff from its approximately seven hundred full-time medical doctors and research scientists.

The success of the Mayos was matched by a monumental modesty on the part of all three of the founders. The elder Mayo often referred to himself as a country doctor from a little town in Minnesota, and the brothers turned a compliment for one into a thanks that started "My brother and I . . ." They rebuffed again and again suggestions that they run for political office. Perhaps that would have been spreading their gifts too thinly, but their influence on the soul of the Mayo Clinic continues.

The clinic admitted 15,000 patients in 1912; now it registers more than 300,000 annually. From the start, the senior Dr. Mayo never refused a patient treatment because of inability to pay, and that spirit has continued to the present day, where treatment precedes discussion of payment.

Dr. Mayo died in 1911 at the age of ninety-two, a victim of a farming accident. His sons died in 1939, one from pneumonia and the other from cancer. The lineage of doctoring continues, although the most recent Mayo doctors have moved elsewhere to practice.

Floods along the Mississippi in 1882 left 85,000 people without homes.

Science on the Move

Scientific discoveries by Midwesterners have happened through both tele-scopes and microscopes. They exist beyond the sight of any naked eye far out in space and deep within our cells. All quite amazing.

• • •

The cyclotron, which has played such a major role in modern physics, was invented by Ernest Lawrence, **a South Dakota native.** He won the Nobel Prize in Physics in 1939 for his accomplishment.

Jerome Friedman, born and educated in Chicago, Illinois, was part of a trio of scientists credited with proving the **existence of quarks.** He won the Nobel Prize for physics in 1990. (Quark is still a silly word.)

James Keeler, LaSalle, Illinois, proved that **Saturn's rings** are not solid but made up of small particles.

George E. Hale, a Chicago, Illinois native, became an astronomer who per-suaded funding sources to pay for the construction of **giant observatories,** including the Yerkes Observatory in Williams Bay, Wisconsin, and Mount Palomar in California.

Clyde Tombaugh was born to a poor family in Streator, Illinois. Without com-pleting college, he was hired by the Lowell Observatory in Arizona. In 1930, **Tombaugh discovered Pluto.** He was awarded a scholarship to the University of Kansas and finished his studies. Now that's a devoted student.

With 750 acres under glass, Ohio is the leading producer of greenhouse vegetables.

John Bardeen from Madison, Wisconsin, is **the first person to win the Nobel Prize for physics twice.** In 1956, he shared it for discovery of the transistor, and in 1972, he won it for work on superconductivity. (Sounds like a synonym for extraordinarily good behavior.)

James A. Van Allen, born in 1914 in Mount Pleasant, Iowa, is a physicist at the University of Iowa and is best known for inventing the cosmic ray detection device which discovered the **radiation belts around the earth,** now called the Van Allen Belts. As it should be.

Illinois scientist Alfred Sturtevant, born in Jacksonville, warned people about the **health hazards of nuclear fallout.**

James Watson was a radio "quiz kid" and child prodigy who later attended the University of Chicago in Chicago, Illinois, and with Francis Crick and Maurice Wilkins discovered the **double helix molecular structure of DNA.**

Robert Millikan, born in Morrison, Illinois, in 1868, studied Greek at Oberlin College but became **enchanted with physics.** He eventually proved Einstein's photoelectric equation and won the Nobel Prize for physics in 1923. He's also known for his efforts to reconcile religion and science.

Enrico Fermi and other physicists produced the **first man-made nuclear reaction** at the University of Chicago in Chicago, Illinois, in December 1942.

Persons aged 25 or over in the Midwest with a bachelor's degree or greater: 32,310,253.

Oh! Those Entrepreneurs

A natural and not surprising result of all that midwestern inventiveness was the formation of businesses—lots and lots of businesses. No doubt a lot more flourished and faded—horseshoeing, hat making, and saloon keepers, to name three.

• • •

Magnate Charles R. Walgreen, of Galesburg, Illinois, was born in 1873 and opened his first drugstore in 1901. We can thank him for innovating the soda fountain and lunch counter in a pharmacy. The idea sank deep into the culture and probably did more to promote varieties of flavors in sodas and varieties of ingredients in sundaes than any other single development. And it may deserve credit for boosting **casual romantic meetings** with "the Coke date." All it took was a bottle and two straws.

As a young salesman in Chicago, Illinois, William Wrigley, Jr., discovered chewing gum to be an effective gimmick to promote what he was supposed to be selling—baking powder. But when people began asking for the gum instead of even pretending they **needed more baking powder,** he took the hint. He started his company in 1893; now Wrigley's sells about half of all the gum sold in America.

Of the Midwest's 599 colleges and universities, 511 are private.

The Ringling brothers spent part of their childhood in the river town of MacGregor, Iowa. Three of them, Alfred, Charles, and John, were born there in 1861, 1863, and 1866. The brothers, impressed by a show traveling along on a Mississippi boat, took up performing in the back yard. Alf, who pursued juggling and acrobatics, could **balance a plow on his chin!** The family moved to Baraboo, Wisconsin, where Albert and Otto were born. In 1884, the boys created a show with a few farm animals. By 1888, the circus could afford to travel by rail around the area. They called themselves "The Ringling Brothers Stupendous Consolidation of Seven Monstrous Shows."

Dr. William Upjohn, **civic leader of Kalamazoo,** Michigan, began a pill-producing business that grew into the well-known major pharmaceutical company.

Hays City, Kansas, was home to an ambitious entrepreneur named Prairie Dog Dave Morrow. Morrow enjoyed a heyday business for a while by domesticating prairie dogs and selling them to tourists and newcomers. Competitors soon cut too deeply into his profits, and he returned to buffalo hunting and succeeded in shooting what many thought was a phantom idea if not altogether a phantom—**an albino buffalo.** Three other white buffalos were killed during the 1870s in the area of the Kansas plains.

Madame C.J. Walker had been a child of slaves. She was widowed at age twenty and her frustration with her poverty drove her to start a business of her own. Like many Black women at the time, she had tried to straighten her hair and failed. But she knew if she could find a safe method, she would be able to make money. She experimented until she found a successful chemical combination and then set up a manufacturing and distribution business. As she traveled the country selling her products, she stopped in Indianapolis, Indiana, and fell in love with the city. She moved her home office and manufacturing plant there. She was **the nation's first Black millionaire.**

"Home on the Range" is Kansas' state song.

Grinding It Out

Food—not just for nutritional needs but for entertainment and pleasure—was transformed into thriving industries. Lucky us.

● ● ●

Orville Redenbacher, Brazil, Indiana, studied agronomy at Purdue University. He and a friend, Charles Bowman, developed the hybrid popcorn that makes such plump kernels. But the hybrid was expensive and no company was interested in investing in the product. Believing that **people would happily pay** for a better popcorn, they began bagging and selling it themselves. Were they ever right! Hunt and Wesson bought the company in 1976 but kept Orville on as a spokesman. He died December 31, 1995.

Kentucky Fried Chicken's Colonel Harland Sanders was born near Henryville, Indiana. Would **Indiana Fried Chicken** have the same ring? (Well, maybe, with some different spices.)

Ray A. Kroc of Oak Park, Illinois, took **the assembly line idea of hamburger preparation** used by Mac's McDonalds in San Bernardino, California, and became the national franchise agent. On April 15, 1955, he opened his own first McDonald's in Des Plaines. I think we know what happened after that.

The Midwest—home to 2 stars who each go by one name: Houdini and Madonna.

Ice cream cones, hamburgers, and crackerjacks are all claimed to be inventions of **Charles E. Menches of Akron, Ohio.** But Wisconsin claims hamburgers, too. (Check out the food chapter for their story.) Menches' crackerjacks was improved by F.W. Rueckheim, Chicago, Illinois, who began the gimmick-in-the-box version of the snack.

Cummins Canning Company in Conneaut, Ohio, was first to pack pumpkin in cans. As a fan of pumpkin bread, pumpkin muffins, **pumpkin ice cream,** and pumpkin anything else, I remain eternally grateful to these innovators.

Harvest news: Illinois is number one in the nation in soybeans, number two in corn and hogs (Iowa is number one), its McLean County is number one in the nation in corn production, its Henry County is number one in hogs, and its Champaign County is number one in soybeans. Unless you've seen it, that's probably **more food than you can imagine.**

The Curtiss Candy Company was founded by Otto Schnering of Chicago, Illinois. Among other favorites, the company sells Baby Ruth, first called **Kandy Kate** but renamed in a contest. The winning name commemorates President Cleveland's oldest daughter who died at age twelve from diphtheria.

Brach is also a Chicago, Illinois, company, founded by Frank Brach. So is Leaf, makers of Chuckles and Milk Duds. And so is the Goelitz Confectionery Company, producers of **the prince of jelly beans**—Jelly Bellys. Chicago may be known for its jazz, its lake, its ribs, and its deep-dish pizza, but now let it be widely known for its candy! The childhood movie experience wouldn't have been the same without it.

Branson, Missouri—the Midwest's answer to Las Vegas, without the gambling.

Fremont, Michigan, is home to the country's largest baby food plant. **It's Gerber's.** Goo.

A clever Elkhart, Indiana, newspaper editor inspired the development of the beloved-by-many Alka Seltzer. The president of Dr. Miles Laboratories (now called Miles Laboratories) was visiting the city one day when "everyone," it seemed, had a cold or the flu. While visiting the newspaper, he noticed that the staff was free of sickness and asked about it. The editor told him that at the first sign of colds, he gave his staff aspirin and bicarbonate of soda. Some **experimenting back at the lab** led to the tablet, released in 1931, that has soothed tummies—and presumably kept colds at bay—for decades.

William Horlick of Racine, Wisconsin, **invented malted milk** in 1882. Thanks.

Miracle Whip was invented by Chicagoan Max Crosset in the early 1940s. He **sold it to Kraft Products for three hundred dollars.** I hope three hundred dollars was precisely what Max wanted and needed, because the dressing has been a Midwest favorite for decades, yielding quite a bit more than three hundred dollars in profits for Kraft.

Margarine, to the chagrin of heartlanders in the dairy business, was invented in 1873. Wisconsinites succeeded in keeping the imitation product out of their state until the 1950s. An early regulation of the butter wannabe was that it be sold colorless. A dab of dye was included so that color could be worked throughout the substance with some patient kneading. The Illinois border had a lively business for **"margarine smugglers."**

Dr. Edward Beeman added the pepsin to gum to aid digestion and incidentally give it a nice flavor. It's the kind of flavor that takes you **back to 1955.**

The average immigrant brought only $12.67 to the United States.

Retail Wizards

Marshall Field, Chicago, Illinois, brought to marketing a number of things we now take for granted—allowing returns, placing a price tag directly on merchandise, opening a bargain basement, and making special efforts to attract female customers. He was very ambitious, moving from clerk at age sixteen to company owner in early adulthood. And he was generous with his success, donating 10,000,000 dollars to establish The Field Museum of Natural History.

Another marketing wonder was the first catalog for shopping by mail. It was a single sheet. Montgomery Ward gets credit for starting this phenomenon in 1872.

The third star in the trio of "early sales *wunderkind* of the Midwest" was Richard Warren Sears. Beginning as a watch salesman, he hired a watch repairman named Alvah C. Roebuck, and they produced a catalog of watches fifteen years after the Ward publication. The first year they kept their business simple and sold only to railway agents, who of course needed to have accurate timepieces. But they decided to try distribution to the public. By 1909, both Sears and Roebuck had quit the mail-order business but Julius Rosenwald of Springfield, Illinois, continued it.

And let us not overlook the maestro of giant chain stores—J.C. Penney, a Missouri farmer, even after opening his first store, which occurred in Wyoming, incidentally.

The Mall of America includes a chapel where couples actually marry.

Getting the Job Done

Midwestern businesses have centered on everything from construction specialties (the firm that built Hoover Dam) to the distribution of mallards (Whistling Wings Duck Hatchery in Illinois). There is much to do and many ambitious souls to tackle the challenges.

With the unlikely name of Grassyfork Fisheries, you might not expect that the business is a major source of goldfish, but the Martinsville, Indiana, company produces **40,000,000 of the shiny fish** annually. They're shipped all over the world.

Jesse Binga, who had been a successful real estate broker in Chicago, Illinois, in the early 1900s founded a bank for Blacks who had migrated north in the 1920s. Provident Hospital in Chicago was started by Dr. Daniel Hale Williams, **a pioneering heart surgeon.** Williams and Binga were among the African-Americans who had lived in Chicago for a generation or two before the great migration occurred; they had time and resources to become established.

John Chapman sold apple seedlings to support his itinerant preaching, which he did as a voluntary missionary for the Swedenborgian Church of New Jerusalem. Tales of his tree planting and **kindness to all of God's creatures** spread up and down the frontier. He died in 1845 and is buried near Fort Wayne, Indiana. An 1871 article in *Harper's* turned him from a footnote in history to the Johnny Appleseed legend we all know.

The Taggart Bread Company of Indianapolis had such success with a one-pound loaf in the first quarter of the nineteenth century that they wanted to sell a one-and-a-half pound loaf. Elmer Cline had the assignment of coming up with a name and decoration for the wrapping. He was inspired by his attendance at **a balloon festival,** which he found to be *wonder*ful. The bread was

The biggest soap factory in the country is in Cincinnati, Ohio.

Wonder, and the colorful dots were balloons. Like the event that inspired it, Wonder Bread took off and has been afloat ever since. Continental Baking bought the trademark in 1925.

Julie Kaufman of Madison, Wisconsin, is the second licensed **chiropractor for animals** in the nation. Her services are much in demand all over the state.

A Montgomery Ward ad man developed the story of **Rudolph, the helpful reindeer,** to help promote a two million piece catalog mailing. Gene Autry wrote the song, and since 1949, Rudolph the Red-Nosed Reindeer has been a standard Christmas tune.

George Francis Train, 1829–1904, made a fortune in shipping, railroading, and street railways. But he was also **a relentless self-promoter, public eccentric, and attention-seeker.** Or maybe he had all that success *because* he was a relentless self-promoter, public eccentric, and attention-seeker.

One of **the richest women in America** is Madonna—born and raised in the Midwest. Yes, she's one of ours, this fabulous, outrageous woman who always invents new ways to attract attention and dazzle sensibilities. Born in Bay City, Michigan, she briefly attended the University of Michigan at Ann Arbor and then took off for New York City with thirty-five dollars in her pocket. She spent half the sum on her first taxi ride.

Madonna Louise Veronica Ciccone was the oldest of six children; her parents were second-generation Italians with big hopes for their offspring. Madonna's mother died when she was very young, and the loss seemed to contribute to a drive that doesn't seem to let up. Madonna has earned at least 20,000,000 dollars a year since 1986, a mere eight years after she landed in the Big Apple. These midwestern women—they do remarkable things.

It was once illegal to impersonate a firefighter in Nebraska, but not now.

Getting There

Wheels have been a key tool of midwestern entrepreneurs. If it hadn't been invented in some earlier era, no doubt some wily Midwesterner would have captured the idea for all the world to share.

• • •

About five thousand cars were "invented" during the heyday of developing horseless carriages. One of the few from Iowa was the Spaulding, which is remembered primarily for racing the "fast" mail train across the state from the Mississippi to the Missouri River in November 1913. **The automobile beat the train** as well as the former record by completing the run in nine hours and fourteen minutes.

The Duryea Motor Wagon won the first auto "contest." Brothers J. Frank and Charles, owned a bike-repair shop in Peoria, Illinois. The contest was actually a show for publicity to promote the possibility of autos replacing horses. The car went forty miles on **a snowy Thanksgiving** in Illinois in 1895. The route was from Jackson Park to Evanston and back, and it took nine hours. As we know, the publicity eventually paid off.

In March 1896, Charles Brady King was the first person to display a horseless carriage to Detroit. King started tinkering with the idea after he saw a combustion engine at the 1893 Columbian Exposition in Chicago. And he wasn't the only one. By summer's end, Henry Ford showed his **gas-powered quadricycle,** and Ransom Olds showed off his.

The U.S.S. Wisconsin was the last battleship ever made; it was launched in 1942.

Detroit, Michigan, claims the first paved concrete highway in the country. The year was 1909, the distance was one mile by twenty-six feet, it took three months to build, and the cost was $13,534.59. **It was probably no accident** that a year earlier Henry Ford began marketing the Model T.

America's first interurban streetcar line traveled between Alexandria and Anderson, Indiana, in 1898. It almost looks like **an alphabetical decision.** What next? Angola? Attica? Auburn?

Walter Percy Chrysler, from Wamego, Kansas, chose a machinist's apprenticeship over a college education and began a journey that led him eventually to reorganize the Maxwell Motor Company. He became president and released Chrysler automobiles in 1924. Among other features, the car had four-wheel hydraulic brakes and a **high-compression engine.** The Chrysler building in New York, which he built in 1929, was a sideline interest; it was the tallest skyscraper there at the time. By 1935, the Chrysler Corporation was the second largest car manufacturer in the United States.

Not all of the early automobile companies were positioned for a bright future. The DeLaura Auto Co. in **Perry, Iowa,** made two cars and went bankrupt.

The Hoosier state had **a thriving auto business** until the 1920s. Over two hundred brands were manufactured there, including the Duesenberg, Auburn, Stutz, and Maxwell. Studebaker was the only one that lasted beyond World War II. A museum in Auburn displays these golden era autos.

The word tractor was made up by a man in Charles City, Iowa, which was the home not only of **tractor companies,** but of a couple of automobile companies, too. W.H. Williams worked for a company that was making something called a "gasoline traction engine." He called them "tractors," and it stuck.

The first African-American mayor of Gary, Indiana, was Richard G. Hatcher.

On the Farm

With agriculture at the center of the Midwest's history and economy, it's no surprise that innovations and various records in farming sparkle through as some of the region's most remarkable accomplishments.

● ● ●

Cyrus McCormick, who was accused of appropriating a lot of other people's inventions, nevertheless successfully put them together in his Virginia reaper. He opened a factory in Chicago, Illinois, in the mid-1850s, and it eventually became one of the **blockbuster farm equipment** companies.

Speaking of blockbuster farm equipment companies, John Deere opened a blacksmith business in Grand Detour, Illinois, in 1837. The constant repair of plows led him to experiment with a broken sawblade of polished steel. The revolutionary aspect of the steel plow was that the metal allowed the sticky black earth to slide back onto the ground; plows made of iron or wood often broke or got stuck from the amount of dirt clinging to the blades. Deere **changed the way America farmed.** Within twenty years, the factory in Moline was producing 10,000 plows annually.

The silhouettes of silos in the Midwest are as common as cows. But once upon a time silage was stored in holes in the ground. It was **a farmer in Spring Grove,** Illinois, who decided to try to avoid the dampness of that method—both from the soil itself and from rain run-off—by storing silage above ground. He took the advice from a Wisconsin scientist who suggested a round construction. It was 1873, when Fred L. Hatch built the first cylindrical silage storage place. It stood on his farm for forty-six years.

Canaan, Indiana, is where Gale Ferris nurtures 40 rare breeds of poultry.

Rural electrification became widespread in 1940. Before that time, windmills were the things that were spread wide as power resources for farms. Batavia, Illinois, was the home of **three windmill companies.**

According to the National Corn Growers Association, Walter Hasselbring of Iroquois County, Illinois, produced **the highest yielding corn crop** seven times between 1975 and 1990. Hasselbring ascribes his success to nitrogen (three hundred pounds per acre), manure (he owns a buffalo herd), and singing—his own—to the corn as he walks through his fields.

A survey done in the 1940s to see which farm tasks were more odious to children found the following. Boys hated, in this order: hauling manure, cleaning out the hen house, milking, and slopping the hogs. Girls hated most: cooking for threshers, washing the cream separator, washing dishes, ironing, and picking chickens. No, you city-types, picking does not mean to select. Check your dictionaries. Definition number three. *Pluck.* Jerking the feathers out. **Dirty, stinky work.** Much nicer indeed to pick your chickens in the supermarket by simply pointing a finger and letting someone else wrap it up.

Kansas author Homer Corey remembers his father **shucking corn barehanded.** The family couldn't afford to buy the flannel mittens that were used at that time by some to protect the skin. The husks, of course, would cut and slice his father's fingers raw. At night before he went to bed, his mother melted tallow and poured it into his father's hands to urge them to heal for the next day's work.

In 1881, B. R. Pierce came from Scotland with cattle to Creston, Illinois. The progeny of the herd still occupy the same farm. So, there you go. **Not all Midwesterners moved.**

Harry S. Truman farmed in Missouri for 11 years before he was active in politics.

Going to the Farm

My grandfather, George Lippold and my grandma, Hertha, raised four sons and my mother on a farm six miles southwest of Avoca, Iowa. Anyone who ever met him would agree that he was a remarkable man. On his business card it read . . . "It is nice to be important but it's more important to be nice." Those were words he lived by.

People would drive for miles to purchase Grandpa's livestock because of his reputation as an honest man who raised only the best stock. Grandpa stood six feet four inches tall, and weighed over three hundred pounds. He had hands as big as a baseball mitt and a booming voice to match. His farm wasn't big, around 340 acres, but on it he, my grandmother, and their four sons raised almost every farm animal you could think of, from purebred Hampshire hogs and Holstein cattle to rat terriers. I suspect his was one of the last farms in the state to use horses as the primary source of power in the fields.

In the summers my brothers and I would find ourselves and our uncles making hay on several different farms in the area. And when it came time to cut Grandpa's hay fields, the neighbors were there to help.

Staying on Grandpa's farm for a few weeks during the summer wasn't necessarily a vacation. On the farm everyone who was able, learned to work at a young age. By the time I was ten, in 1955 or so, I was put to work in the fields.

After a breakfast of Grandma's pancakes, eggs, bacon, sausage, and toast, preceded by the daily chores, we would head for the haying fields. Grandpa would sometimes tie us onto the seat because our day started at sun-up, and the constant rhythm of the mower blades would rock us to sleep. The horses knew their job and continued mowing.

Asbestos, the great insulator, was developed by Charles C. Hill in Alexandria, Indiana.

We usually didn't come in until the end of the day. Grandma would bring a lunch to the field, and a mid-afternoon break brought more sandwiches, cookies and Kool-Aid. It was usually dark by the time we came in, fed all the livestock, milked the cows again, and stumbled to the house for supper, as it was called on the farm.

The farm house was just that, a farm house. It wasn't fancy. It wasn't even pretty. The only room in the house that had carpeting was the living room or parlor, and it was never used unless there was company or a special occasion. The real center of social activity on Grandpa's farm was the basement. And it really was a basement. The concrete floor was the only improvement made since the house was built.

Outside access to the basement stairs was from a door on the south side of the house. Muddy boots and work shoes were removed there, and several wooden pegs at the foot of the stairs collected jackets and caps in the winter. A gun rack in one corner displayed a couple of shotguns and a rifle or two. Hunting was a regular topic of discussion among my uncles during meals.

After supper we would sit around the table for a while talking about the day's events or tomorrow's plans, or telling jokes, or listening to one of my uncles relate a past episode about how tough he had it when he was a kid growing up on the farm. My uncles were great story-tellers.

By nine o'clock or earlier many nights, we were ready to call it a day. There was no TV on the farm but we would have been too tired to watch it anyway. Before the sun was up the next day, our wake-up call would come in the form of Grandpa's voice booming through the floor register and everything would start over again.

Dennis Schneider
Johnston, Iowa

In the "good old days," plasterers and blacksmiths earned about $1.25 to $2.00 per day.

First, Biggest, Greatest

Anabella Bobb Mansfield (1846–1911) born near Burlington, Iowa, was **the first woman admitted to the practice of law** in the United States.

The world's largest basket is on display at Longaberger Baskets in Zanesville, Ohio. Employees worked on the basket for two thousand hours. It's forty-eight feet long, eleven feet wide, and twenty-three feet tall, and made of hardwood sugar maple. Do you suppose one might borrow it for a little **May Day surprise** for a friend?

The first patent granted for **a vending machine** that dispenses liquid went to—ta da!—Minnesotan William Henry H. Fruen on December 16, 1884.

The first correspondence course in **tree surgery** was begun by the Davey Tree Expert Company in Kent, Ohio, in 1914.

University of Michigan in Ann Arbor, Michigan, offered the first full course in forestry at a university. **The year was 1881.** When you think of the name of the city, how could it have been any other way. Arbor? Bower? Tree? Forest? With me on this one?

Katie Beatrice Hall of Gary was **Indiana's first Black woman elected to U.S. Congress** from that state.

The first commercial crop-dusting company** was begun by C.E. Woolman, Bloomington, Indiana. The company eventually became Delta Air Lines. Talk about expansion and growth.

Shirley Plume, an Oglala Sioux from North Dakota, was the first Native American selected as a superintendent of an agency of the Bureau of Indian

From April 1994–1995, 25% of Midwesterners had saved 0 dollars toward retirement.

Affairs. She performed her job for the **Standing Rock Agency** at Fort Yates, North Dakota.

It might seem surprising that the first Arab-American elected to the U.S. Senate came from the Midwest and was in fact born in Wood, South Dakota. His name was **James Abourezk.** He championed Native American rights and frequently led opposition to the Nixon Administration.

Ben Reifel (1906–1990) was born near Parmalee, South Dakota. He was a **Brule Sioux** and the only Native American member of Congress in the post-World War II era.

In 1956 Shirley S. Abrahamson, who was first in her class in the Indiana Law School, was advised that she may as well look for a job as a law librarian because **so few law firms were willing to hire women.** She got her true rewards in 1976 when she became the first woman justice on the Wisconsin Supreme Court.

It would of course be in a city named Holland, located in Michigan along the lakeshore, that Americans would find the only **wooden shoe factory** in the nation.

The first patent for chewing gum** was issued in 1869 to W.F. Semple of Mount Vernon, Ohio.

Ernest Pflueger, Akron, Ohio, invented **artificial fish bait** in 1880. One wonders what the inspiration was—weather too inclement for worm-digging? Broken spade? Aversion for touching worms? Animal rights advocate, at least for the lowly ones? Hmmm.

From April 1994–1995, 14% of Midwesterners had saved over $10,000 for retirement.

The first **baby-sitters' insurance policy** was granted by the American Associated Insurance Companies in St. Louis, Missouri, on January 26, 1950. The policy protected against fraud and dishonesty. I can't say if it protected parents, sitters, or babies.

The **first surgical operation,** which was for gallstones, was conducted in Indianapolis in 1867 by a Dr. J.S. Bobbs.

Arthur P. Warner, Wisconsin's first pilot, assembled and then flew the first commercially built airplane in the country. **The flight occurred in Beloit.** I don't know how large it was or how long it flew. So much to learn, so little time.

In an autumn in Trenton, Michigan, around 1925 or so, **the first traffic lines** were painted on roads to designate lanes. The name was "center line safety stripe."

Ohio boasts the **first brick pavement on a rural road.** The 7.93-mile stretch was constructed in 1895.

June 1926 marked the **beginning of the sale of electric toasters**. It happened in the land where people not only love but need warm bread—Minneapolis, Minnesota. The device had one handle to lower the bread and another to serve as timer. Marketed under the name of Toastmaster, the device cost $13.50.

More than 50 insurance companies have their home offices in Des Moines, Iowa.

Our Wonderful Food

Roast Beef, Medium, is not only a food. It is a philosophy.
Seated at Life's Dining Table, with the menu of Morals
before you, your eye wanders a bit over the entrees,
the hors d'oeuvres, and the things à la *though you know that*
Roast Beef, Medium, is safe and sane, and sure.

– Edna Ferber (1887–1968)

When you think of midwestern food, what comes to mind? Is it the quirky way beef was prepared in your old neighborhood? Sloppy Joes, Maid-Rites, square burgers, or endless mounds of beef-noodle casserole. Is it something cold and jiggly or might it be ribs dripping with barbecue sauce, perhaps tapioca, gravy, those fresh garden vegetables, or tart, crisp apples? Growing up midwestern means growing up with hearty food—much of it coming right out of the heartland. And it also means eating ethnic specialties cooked from recipes from past generations.

Food is a basic part of any culture; it's no wonder that immigrants, coming to a new land where other foods are available, continue to eat the dishes they know and love (in the same way perhaps that as adults we return to foods that were favorites when we were children). What was central to palates in one community was often unpronounceable to neighbors a few miles away. Ethnic dishes, prepared from generally unavailable ingredients or using common ingredients in an unusual way, supplied an echo of the immigrants' homelands. Cooking pots and ovens around the Midwest were the source of a range of odors. Consider the following: sauerkraut and sauerbraten (German), fish puddings and *bakkels* (Scandinavian), ravioli and *gnocchi* (Italian), goulash and *galuska* (Hungarian), and gyros and *moussaka* (Greek), chop suey and fried rice (Chinese), or borscht and *bitochky smetance* (Armenian and Russian). And that, of course, is just a start.

The hundreds of pockets of immigrants in the Midwest are reflected throughout the area in a vast variety of foods. Examining how one food—bread, for example—is preferred and prepared by people in one medium-sized city would illustrate a range of sweet, sour, salty, yeasty, short, fried, baked, or stuffed breads, to say nothing of the variety of shapes. Food preparation and eating habits, too, change over time and place because of cooking methods and available ingredients, and they change because of exposure to the tastes of others. Many items have become so much a part of the homogenized American diet—sausage, olive oil, macaroni, hot cakes—that we have to pause to think of their original home place. Nevertheless, many midwestern dishes retain their integrity and uniqueness, whether they're cooked at home or in home-grown restaurants. There is much to choose from, many tastes to enjoy. It would take months to eat your way from one edge of the Midwest to the other.

Beyond the regional foods are those enjoyed by members of a particular ethnic group or even by a particular family; these dishes are made "kitchen by kitchen" or—one is tempted to say—grandmother by grandmother. Even though they're not widely available, recipes for many esoteric ethnic foods can be found in cookbooks produced by women's clubs or churches. And some recipes exist only in our own recipe boxes, sent by a mother or aunt or grandfather who "wanted us to have the recipe."

Meanwhile, we've come to know better than we may have wanted to know that we are—in terms of fat and fiber as well as vitamins and minerals—what we eat. The prosperous midwestern soil yields staples galore: corn, pork, cream, beef, cheese, cream, butter, beer, cream, flour, cereals, cream, cherries, apples, cream, and blueberries. "Hearty" is the common denominator. The farmers needed those carbohydrates to get their fieldwork and housework done. And so the legacy of "hearty," or "heavy" if you insist, food stays with us.

But something else happens annually in the Midwest that counterbalances the delicious pork gravy, the Dutch Apple pies, the scalloped corn and potatoes, and the beef goulash. That "something" is gardens. The black, rich soil invites even the most naive gardener to toss in a few tomato seeds. The reward of fresh carrots, lettuce, cucumbers, peas, radishes, zucchini, and squash are a welcome change of diet. For those who don't have their own gardens, farmers' markets beckon Midwesterners on Saturday mornings in cities and towns throughout the twelve states. Ambitious shoppers buy bagfuls and freeze or can the produce against the coming season. The rest of us indulge in the summer's flavor-rich, sweet, juicy tomatoes and the sweet corn picked just hours earlier.

Our heritage connects us not only to the food itself, but to our gardens and markets, to varied preparations, and to the many customs and ceremonies of eating. All of these things contribute to who we are, food-wise. And although we share with the rest of the country the instant or at least easy open-and-eat foods-of-convenience, when there's time to cook, or when it's a holiday, we often drift back to the foods we loved as children—the foods that require specific and sometimes elaborate preparations. Our longings for food from the past dictate menus for special days or for "comfort" snacks. Perhaps the bits that follow here will take you back. Enjoy!

Food, Glorious, Abundant Food

Lucky, lucky us. The Midwest has been called the breadbasket of the world, and, here we are, right in the middle of it. The abundant products of the rich soil have been matched by a generosity of servings—the all-you-can-eat meals at restaurants flourish in the Midwest—that grew out of the 1800s. In a time when every sort of service had a price tag, travelers found it noteworthy that meals were usually included in the cost of a hotel room.

• • •

When author Harriet Martineau traveled to the Midwest in the 1800s, she tried to buy **wild strawberries** from children who were gathering them. They insisted on giving them to her and would take no money. She found this so surprising that she wrote she had glimpsed "the end of the world; or rather, perhaps, the beginning of another and a better."

Although some early settlers had rough years as they began their home-steading, and the **dustbowl years** and Depression took their toll, many mid-western farms survived because of their gardens. If a family was lucky enough to have abundant crops, all ate well.

Genuine tea was expensive and difficult to obtain on the frontier. Substitute drinks included parched and ground wheat or grub hyson, which was made of **sycamore chips** and red-root leaves (sometimes dried in a Dutch oven and then pulverized). The brew was sweetened with honey. That would certainly fall into the category of "making do."

In Xenia, Ohio, it's against the law to spit into a salad bar. Thank goodness.

City-dwellers' appetite for prairie chickens meant that the birds disappeared in large numbers very quickly. In 1871, the Chicago, Illinois, meat markets sold more than **half a million prairie chickens.** In New York City in 1878 it was reported that two thousand a day were sold during the Christmas season.

Update: **Wisconsin prairie chickens** are on the rebound thanks to a group of concerned bird lovers.

Class consciousness about food entered the midwestern psyche in terms of acceptable meats. Beef and pork were the desirable meats in the early 1800s, and it was said that if Midwesterners couldn't get these meats, they would **live on cornbread** for a month rather than eat mutton or veal, rabbit, or wild fowl.

A typical breakfast aboard a Mississippi steamboat might include tea, coffee, eggs, **salted mackerel,** mush, beefsteaks, hot rolls, corn cakes, molasses, and more. As if anyone needed more!

Charles Dickens described a supper he witnessed in St. Louis, Missouri, when he was visiting America in the 1830s. The meal included tea, coffee, bread, butter, salmon, shad, liver, steak, potatoes, pickles, ham, chops, **black puddings,** and sausages. Remarkable as it was, even more remarkable to him was that precisely the same items appeared for breakfast the next morning, and for lunch, minus the tea and coffee. He was taken aback to see all of it mixed up on the plates as well. Welcome to America—buffet heaven.

Battle Creek, Michigan, produces more cereal than any other city on earth.

At the midwestern long table, some basic foods dominated. Cream, sugar, beef, potatoes, pork, pies, puddings, cakes, pickles and preserves. No exotic spices or herbs. **Salt and pepper held sway**. All foods were identifiable, with the exception of the contents of a pudding, and all of it was served ready-to-eat; bread was sliced, any fruits that may have demanded time-consuming peeling had been baked into a pie.

Vegetables were in short supply and were thought to be rather tasteless. Francis Trollope, who **loved to attack the interior** of the United States, wondered if a "milder sun and cooler air" weren't better for gardens. Tsk tsk.

In the lumbercamps in Michigan, there was a sign posted:
"NO TALKING AT THE TABLE."

Farmers' markets are making a comeback in many metropolitan areas, but there are some parts of the country where they've never gone out of fashion. Starting with lettuce in early summer and continuing until late fall and the last pumpkins, farmers' markets offer **fresh sweet corn,** raspberries at half the cost of "Imports," and, in many areas, brown-shelled eggs, and breads that might still be warm from the oven.

The seeds of Kansas' position as a leader in wheat production were planted in 1874, when **Russian Mennonites** settled in the area with their Turkey Red Wheat. The wheat was ideal for the Kansas soil and climate.

Beans and salt pork (usually the sowbelly) were a common meal for the lumberjacks, topped off with frycakes for dessert. Perhaps it's noteworthy that the lumberjacks were **rarely ill.** Perhaps. Maybe it was the fresh air and hard work. Maybe it was lucky genes. Could it have been salt pork?

Carl Sandburg's grandmother made a memorable beverage—dandelion wine.

Sunday Food

My father is a Baptist minister and we used to travel all over Indiana back in the late 1950s in a tan-and-white Chevy. We would caravan to small Black churches in little towns and be greeted by large robust women with big bosoms. They had their Sunday dresses on under aprons, and slippers on their feet.

They would serve us fried chicken, ham, macaroni and cheese, greens, corn, green beans, and corn bread, or rolls, pies, cakes, and sometimes homemade ice cream. They piled our plates high with food.

We ate in small dank basements that had cement floors and pipes running across the ceiling and Sunday school posters and pictures of a serene Jesus looking heavenward. If it was summer, tables were often set up outside under trees. We would eat, and then while the hosts cleaned up, the choir practiced and we ran around playing with the kids, constantly being warned not to get dirty.

Then those women would take off their aprons and slippers and put on their hats and shoes for evening service.

On the way back home, my Dad would turn on the radio, and my two sisters and I would sit in the back seat listening to the crackle of the radio, or sometimes my Dad and Mom would tell us stories about when they were kids, or sometimes we would be lulled to sleep by the murmurings of their voices as they talked to each other.

I have moved back to my hometown with my family, and I sing in the choir and travel with my children to some of those same churches today where I used to listen to music and eat that amazing food.

Jolene Wright
Bloomington, Indiana

Corn is Ohio's top farm crop; 22% of all farm receipts are from corn.

Table Manners

Eating in the Midwest was a very democratic experience. In public places, food was served at long tables in what we now call family-style dining. There was no way for one person to expect or demand better service or finer fare than anyone else at the table. This irked some of the nineteenth century travelers. Class-conscious Frances Trollope, mother of novelist Anthony, objected strenuously to American dining habits, describing a meal as an "ordeal" during which she couldn't help but "feel repugnance." Sorry, Fanny. Lighten up.

The fact is that like other social interactions, table manners were redefined in the Midwest to accommodate living conditions. The results often reflected the goal: Eat up and get back to work.

• • •

Sopping—dipping bread in the communal pot of meat and vegetable juices—was an acceptable method of eating. It was, however, **considered rude** to wipe one's fingers on either the bread or the table cloth. So, did everyone have napkins or were they to wipe their hands on their clothes? Iowans in "better circles" elevated the practice by introducing forks. (Dunking one's donuts or cinnamon toast is still a beloved custom in some midwestern homes.)

"Speed-eating" seemed to be a natural characteristic of the early Midwest. Travelers to the region noted repeatedly that twenty minutes was all the time allotted for a day's main meal, and **even on a steamboat,** most people were done in ten or fifteen minutes. With nothing pressing, no one is quite sure why the pressure to eat quickly—and without talking—became such a strong custom.

Spiced Red Cabbage is a popular Dutch treat.

There was another surprise at the midwestern table and that was **great civility.** Words spoken to a waiter or to the innkeeper were kept in a low tone, and there were never complaints about the food. It may have been left on the plate, but no one demanded a replacement or complained about its preparation. Somehow I don't think that Fanny Trollope would be so soft-spoken.

Another element of early midwestern food was the timing. Travelers reported up to **fourteen dishes on the table at once.** At once. Dishes didn't arrive by courses but all together. Some travelers wished their plates had been warmed or a printed menu available to make choices from, but not in the Midwest. Instead, there was democracy at the table. Chow down.

Finally, mealtime democratization meant serving all kinds of foods for all kinds of meals. Thus hotcakes were served for dinner and two-inch-thick beefsteaks for breakfast. And we still have **"Pancake Suppers"** all over the Midwest (sometimes offered from 8:00 A.M. to 8:00 P.M.), and our cousins on the coasts smile, or laugh hysterically, when they hear about this.

And now a word from one of our own . . .

While I have found a home and happiness here in Napa Valley, my roots were in the Iron Range of Minnesota. My immigrant parents ran a grocery store and boarding house—from that experience I learned that you can preserve a warm and hospitable quality of life even in a spare environment. There was always good food and wine at the table and a happy welcome to those who shared our meals. My mother was an exceptional cook, which united not only the family, but many friends. It was this sense of family and "the good table" that I brought to California.

— ROBERT MONDAVI, Winemaker

Paprika is a Hungarian spice. Terrific on chicken or veal.

Sledding and More

Each year, in my hometown in Ohio, my friend Bethany invited several school chums to her house in the country for a day of "sledding" or ice-skating. As for me, there was always great anticipation especially for the sledding. That's because at Bethany's winter parties, sledding was a little different.

We'd all get layered and bundled, and head out to find Bethany's older brother, Tim, sitting astride an old red tractor, revving the engine. Behind the tractor was hitched the "sled," which actually was more like a wagon without the wheels.

"All aboard!" Tim would call out.

Gleefully, we did as he said, feeling giddy while at the same time a little silly. Then Tim would step on the gas and with a jolt, we were off. Of course, most of the fun was being knocked about a bit as the sled bumped and swooshed along, sometimes at what seemed like dizzying speeds. Also fun was the "accidental" fall off the sled into the deep and undisturbed snow. The "fall" was then usually followed by a comedic chase of the sled and its merry band, and it ended with a grand leap back on. Some were better at it than others, and usually those most skilled tried to pelt as many as possible with the cold snow as they tumbled onto the heap of laughing friends.

When it was over, we headed back to Bethany's home to warm ourselves at the huge fireplace. Bethany's mother would bring out hot chocolate and Bethany offered us "Whoopie Pies" (cookies with a sugar/cocoa filling). While we sipped, munched, and thawed out, we talked school and about our lives after high school.

Lee McCrillis
Bloomington, Indiana

Persimmons grow in southern Indiana; the fruit sometimes goes into ice cream.

Midwestern Specialties

It is surprising and satisfying that, while our nationally homogenized country has many products and restaurants that thrive from one border to the other, we continue to have regional foods. They probably exist for three primary reasons—the ethnic groups who settled the area, the food types that were favored by the climate, and the work and life habits that dictated nutritional needs. Rationalizing aside, the foods often hearken to some of our happiest eating memories. Read on.

• • •

More French fries are **consumed in the Midwest** than in any other part of the country. And deep in our happy though perhaps clogging hearts, we're a little proud of it, I suspect.

Nut Goodies, that candy bar with a white center surrounded by peanuts and chocolate is **available only in Minnesota,** so stock up when you get the chance.

There's a rumor that some people in the Midwest eat **French fried cheese curds.** I was unable to learn more.

Ice cream and ice water were both popular in the early days of the Midwest. Writer Milton Mackie reported that at a **St. Louis hotel** in 1864, guests were handed slabs of ice cream that reminded him of "the vastness of the prairie." And ice water appeared in pitchers at the long table three times a day. Quite impressive.

In June of 1994, a Gallup survey revealed that of Midwesterners who drink alcoholic beverages, fifty-six percent of them prefer beer to other forms of alcohol, twenty-three percent of them prefer wine, and sixteen percent name

More beer is consumed in Wisconsin than in any other state.

hard liquor as their preference. A slight sixteen percent **would favor prohibition** and a rousing eighty-four percent would oppose it. So the fact that seventy-three percent of Midwesterners drink alcohol, which is the highest percentage by geographical zone in the country, isn't such a surprise. Do you suppose that our high percentage of beer-loving, German immigrants has something to do with the figures?

Is Kansas City barbecue praised often enough? A secret of the meat is a combination of smoking and **long, slow cooking** rather than grilling. Sauce is often served on the side. And the inside word is that the process requires a grill top with vents.

Hot dogs have remained a long-time favorite in the Midwest, partly because of the heritage from several ethnic groups. In Kansas City, hot dogs are topped with steamed onions and **yellow mustard.** In Chicago, the tradition is yellow mustard, chopped raw onion, sweet relish, dill pickles, tomato, and celery salt on a poppyseed bun. Dijon mustard appears on a lot of tables, too, but often with an embarrassed chuckle that is laughter's equivalent of "get real."

A recipe for **sour cream sugar cookies** probably exists in every church cookbook ever compiled in the Midwest. And it's a good thing, too.

Sugar pies are made from left-over crusts filled with milk or **cream and sugar** and thickened with flour. Basic, sweet, and no doubt comforting.

The Midwest's sweet tooth shows even in their salad dressing. **French dressing** is the most popular.

Pickled pigs' feet. Need I say more?

Maytag bleu cheese is said to be better than Roquefort and Stilton; it's made by one of the Maytag sons from Maytag Appliances in Newton, Iowa, who wanted to use the milk from his **Holstein-Friesian cows.**

Then there was the Iowan who said when he was growing up in the 1950s he always thought that **mayonnaise was an imitator** of Miracle Whip.

Midwestern cole slaw is **generally creamy** and often, though not necessarily, sweet.

Innovative uses of the resources in the kitchen included early German and Scandinavian settlers using **violet blossoms in vinegar.**

Rhubarb is a favorite midwestern vegetable. Yes, a vegetable, and like that other favored vegetable—pumpkin, **rhubarb makes a dandy pie.** And jelly and sauce and cobbler and crunch. Besides the basic fruit-sugar-flour recipe, rhubarb is a great addition to a chess pie, which provides the rhubarb with a sweetened egg base that is flavored with cinnamon. Another diehard way to eat rhubarb is fresh-plucked from the ground. Even when the stalks are slender, it'll pucker your lips, but it's something you have to do. The truly too-sour varieties demand a dip into a saucer of sugar. Midwestern childhood includes this treat as part of growing up.

Burgoo is a slow-cooking, savory French stew, that was highly popular in Morgan, Jersey, Greene, and Macoupin counties in southern Illinois. When writer Nels Algren, Chicago, Illinois, was assigned to a WPA project of **investigating ethnic foods** in the Midwest, he reported on what was popular and sometimes he offered recipes. He found one for modern burgoo from an Armenian recipe. The book containing his findings is called *America Eats.*

Onion and butter sandwiches, or in a pinch, radish and butter. Nothing like it.

The Mississippi River feeds the people who live on both sides with catfish. The catfish are often dipped in a cornmeal batter and fried. Missouri is home to **a love for molasses,** and one way it's eaten is in molasses cornmeal pancakes. And more molasses might be poured on them for eating. What do molasses and catfish have in common? Well, try adding a tad of molasses to the catfish batter and you'll find out for yourself.

Racine, Wisconsin, is known for many things, but one of the tastiest is a pastry. Bakers ship the **Danish kringles**—delectable coffee cakes—all over the world.

The cooks must have been having **a stubborn spell** to cause the Iowa legislature to resolve that cornbread should be served in the legislature's cafeteria.

Dumplings are **another midwestern favorite,** especially when served with chicken.

The black walnuts that grow in several midwestern states are **hard to crack.** A vice or a sledge hammer are often prescribed, but the rewards are worth it for nut lovers. The nutmeat is sometimes baked into a bread that also includes onions. (But let's face it. You really have to like these things. It takes hours to get a cup, and if you forget to wear gloves, your hands will be stained for a week. Also, tomato plants won't grow in the vicinity of a black walnut tree. Just so you know the down side, too.)

Chili in the Midwest is served chock-full of **hearty beans** in the north and often over some kind of pasta or spaghetti in the south and eastern areas.

Another traditional way to fry fish is in a **beer batter.** Ask Wisconsinites about this.

Getting hungry yet?

Hunting the Elusive Mushroom

Part 1

A woman who lives now in Northern California remembers fondly some "gourmet mushroom" moments from her childhood. "Every spring my father and Uncle Don would leave early in the morning, after a rain, to go mushroom hunting," she reported. "They had special spots in the woods surrounding our small town where they went to find morel mushrooms. Usually they returned with several grocery bags overflowing with morel mushrooms—in all sizes and shapes." The harvest created great excitement in their household, because her mother would then soak them in water, dust them with flour and fry them in fresh, sweet butter. The family ate an entire meal consisting of mushrooms. What good fortune. She said she smiles and recalls those early Wisconsin springs every time she sees morels in her local specialty produce market, priced at twenty-five dollars or more a pound!

Part 2

And another morel mushroom tale surrounds a champion mushroomer, whom we'll call John. He is known for his skill in finding the delectable fungi, but he is just as well known for keeping the secret of his fruitful locations. He held his friends at bay for years, and for years they accepted it, but they finally came up with a classic midwestern solution. One spring day, John prepared for a hunt and went out to his car. What did he find but several of his friends, sitting in their cars, ready and waiting to be led to the fertile spot. The fable has become legendary.

A festive evening from decades ago was a taffy pull.

Delicacies from the Old Country

What good fortune that family recipes are so cherished. And three cheers for the annual festivals and rare restaurants that serve truly unique ethnic dishes. This brief section can be expanded by hundreds and thousands of family secrets. Check with the library. Call your aunt.

Russians in Lincoln, Nebraska, like krautrance, where cabbage and meat are rolled in a wheat flour dough and baked; rawnze—cherries or apples spread on **a piece of dough,** the corners of which are folded together and baked; and pigs in a blanket, Russian-style—meatballs rolled in cabbage leaves and boiled.

In St. Paul, Minnesota, French settlers shared with the Sioux the custom of paying visits on New Year's Day to collect **wine, cakes, and kisses.** They called it Kissing Day.

At the Amana colonies, in Iowa, from prior to 1850 until the communal kitchens closed several decades later, the fine art of bread-baking was practiced with care. A wood-heated oven **baked a hundred loaves,** which the women removed with long wooden paddles. The bread was ready when all the wood— the same number of pieces each time—had finished burning.

Swedes brought the smorgasbord to America. Smorgasbord was first a type of pot luck, with specialties brought by the women who came. After restaurants took over the idea, homemakers unfortunately grew too intimidated by the **showy displays** to continue the tradition in quite the same way. Pot lucks, however, continue to the present day.

Home-made popcorn balls were hot and needed lots of hands to work fast.

The Czechs of Minnesota, Nebraska, and Iowa still enjoy kolacky or kolaches. These tender rolls have center fillings made with fruit—often cherries or prunes—or poppyseeds. **Some Czechs still grow their own poppies.**

An Itoo menu, served by the Lebanese in Peoria, Illinois, includes djaaj, mahshi, kebba, mihshie djaga, mihshie kussa, mishie, malfoof, loubia, and slotta. The ingredients for these dishes are beef, varied spices, crushed wheat, lamb, chicken, **a vegetable similar to a cucumber,** string beans, cabbage, salad vegetables, succulent sauces, and a bread that is eased into its shape by being gently stretched over a clean sheet on top of soft comforters. Aren't you finding this educational?

Lefse is an innocuous way to use up boiled potatoes. Mash then, mix with flour, roll as thin as a heavy cabbage leaf, and "fry" on a griddle using no fat. You get **a thin, soft accompaniment for meals.** Typically, Norwegian adults like to roll it up with lutefisk and peas inside. Children often prefer butter and sugar inside. This includes some grown-up children.

Greek honey cake was promoted by Chicago's Greek population, and now **baklava, as it is called,** can be found in many bakeries alongside muffins and cookies.

Rommegrot, a Norwegian pudding of sorts is a treat for home but also is traditionally served after Norwegian weddings. Made from **boiled cream,** flour, and salt, it is poured hot onto a plate where a big pat of butter melts in its middle. Sprinkle generously with cinnamon and sugar and enjoy.

Many Jewish foods have strong traditional ties to holidays. On Purim, the celebration of the death of Haman, who had decreed that all Jews should die, Hamantaschen are served. Hamantaschen, **small three-corner cakes** that commemorate the shape of Haman's pockets, are eaten all over the world. Jews also exchange gifts of food on Purim, a tradition that began because some Jews

Be impressed! 42 wineries in Ohio produce 1,700,000 million gallons a year.

could not afford the ingredients for the cakes, and it was believed that none should have to go without.

The most popular Polish contribution to midwestern cuisine is kielbasa, a sausage that **can be eaten hot or cold.** Khlodnik—a soup of meat, beet tops, sour cream and hard-boiled eggs, fish, and cucumber—is another favorite.

Charchouka, an African dish, is cooked in **individual casseroles** and features vegetables and hot peppers, plus an egg.

Germany's spaetzle is sometimes served as **a substitute for potatoes.** The dough can be pushed through a colander into boiling water and cooked immediately or allowed to chill for later frying. Butter is key at some point—either freshly drizzled on the boiled version or used to fry the chilled version. How can you go wrong?

The Germans like to have some of their favorite ingredients not only between slices of bread but cooked right inside, too. Consider sauerkraut and rye bread or onion and dill bread. **Ya, ya.**

Swedish rice pudding with lingonberry sauce was a traditional food that **moved to the Midwest with the Scandinavians.** Norwegians also served the sauce with their dessert pancakes, which are similar to crêpes. Tasty.

Bread and butter pudding cake is **another traditional Scandinavian sweet,** but I don't know if it's more bread, more pudding, or more cake.

Farfel is a dry small noodle used in Jewish casseroles and soups.

German potato salad is a staple in the Midwest. It has two characteristics: It is served warm and it **includes bleu cheese.**

And another undeniably German treat is **sauerkaut chocolate cake.** The cabbage holds moisture like other canned fruits might. The cake doesn't taste "sauer," I'm told. And if you don't think about sauerkraut when you eat it, you might enjoy it quite a lot.

Kuchen wraps its ingredients inside a **sweet and light** crust. Fillings are sweetened cottage cheese or fruit.

Coffee is a favorite of Scandinavians, and they became skilled at developing pastries worthy of dunking. A Dutch one resembles donut holes and is called oliebollen, which sounds like **the plop of a round sweet** into a hot cup of coffee.

Mineral Point, Wisconsin, was once a mining center populated by Cornish people. It was settled in 1932, but by 1935, with the mines nearly abandoned, its buildings were crumbling. Women trying to save the main building found Charles Curtis, an eighty-three-year-old, who had been the chief stonemason for Frank Lloyd Wright. Curtis agreed to restore the building, and the **women raised the funds,** partly through the sale of Cornish pastries—small pies of beef, potato and onion. The effort was a success. Amazing what can be done with bake sales.

Welsh contributions to America included seed cake and froise, a griddle tea cake.

A Cheesy Tale

From *The Story of Monroe: Its Past And Its Progress Toward the Present,* by E.C. Hamilton

ONE DAY IN 1873, the future of Monroe, Wisconsin, as a major cheese force in the Midwest, was brought into sharp focus.

Apparently several people "with sensitive noses" in the town had complained about the "aromatic" Limburger cheese being hauled by the wagonloads through town to the railroads. (One doesn't need to have too sensitive a nose to notice that odor; in fact a good head-cold couldn't block the Limburger "aroma.")

Three of the town fathers, who had emigrated from Switzerland, consulted on the matter. One of the leaders, Arabut Ludlow, was well aware of the growing flood of healthy bank drafts from eastern buyers being handled at the local bank. Consequently, he had little sympathy for the indignant sniffers. The men talked and came up with a novel solution. They arranged for *all* cheese-producing farmers to bring their wagonloads on a certain day, gathering first at Ludlow's farm where they could form a parade into town to line up around the Courthouse park.

The day came and the wafting wagons attracted a host of curious spectators. When everyone had settled down, Ludlow presented a very terse speech:

"Ladies and Gentlemen: This smelling cheese came into Green County to stay and will make our county famous."

There was no more talk about "offensive" aroma and Monroe's first "Cheese Days" Festival was an eminent (if also an emanating) success.

Each American farmer produces enough food to feed 128 people.

The Kellogg Boys

HOW DO YOU PERSUADE people that there's a better breakfast than ham, sausage, eggs, fried potatoes, and other such heart-stoppers? The answer is Corn Flakes, or at least it was in the 1920s at John Kellogg's sanitarium.

It wouldn't be a complete breakfast story without the story of the Kellogg brothers. They were an unusual pair. John became a doctor and Will dropped out of high school to work. John had intense drive, and it was he who devised what would become Corn Flakes. But Will, younger by eight years, had his own ambitions. It was he who ended up with the Kellogg empire.

John, following the family's spiritual path, became a staff member at the Western Health Reform Institute, which had been established by Seventh Day Adventists. It was a struggling enterprise, but John hired other medical professionals, changed the name to the Battle Creek Sanitarium, and offered a program in healthful living that brought in a well-paying clientele, attracting the likes of John D. Rockefeller and Henry Ford. At the time—the turn of the century—water cures and health spas were in vogue, which helped popularize the venture. Clients cheerfully underwent a change of life, at least for a few weeks; in addition to a strict regimen, clients enjoyed distractions such as plays, picnics, lectures, and cooking classes. All of these activities were designed to improve their health, keep them on a vegetarian diet, and keep their minds off the liquor, coffee, and tobacco that they had left behind, at least temporarily.

Although Kellogg's business was a big success, he never stopped trying to improve it. Part of his effort had to do with finding substitutes for what people were used to eating. The idea of cooking a grain and

More than 300 breweries have opened in Wisconsin since 1840—and some have closed.

then mashing it into a flake was tried by Henry D. Perky of Denver, Colorado, but it met with a different success: He eventually developed shredded wheat. Kellogg experimented with the idea, and said he dreamed, literally, of a solution where he forced cooked wheat through his wife's dough flattener. When he flicked off the paste, he saw the beginning of wheat flakes. Brother Will continued to experiment with another grain, and three years later he'd perfected corn flakes.

Meanwhile, another product was developed by C. W. Post, who had been a patient in the sanitarium. His experiments resulted in the coffee substitute, Postum, and three years later, in 1898, he perfected Grape Nuts. The excitement about developing breakfast cereals is evident from the fact that in 1901 alone, when Battle Creek had a population of 30,000 people, forty companies were incorporated with the stated purpose of manufacturing wheat flakes.

But back at the Kellogg domain, while John focused on the sanitarium, Will grew more and more interested in promoting cereal. In 1906, the year The Battle Creek Toasted Corn Flake Company was founded, Will took out a full-page ad in *The Ladies Home Journal*; business skyrocketed to three thousand cases a day. Within a few years, because of previous arrangements he and his brother had made, Will owned the majority of stock. In 1925, Will started a foundation with the company's profits. It bears Will's name, and is one of the most active humanitarian foundations in the country.

Ironically, as Will's star rose, John's sank. The sanitarium failed as the idea of health spas gave way to the harder times of the Depression and to other forms of health care. Both men lived into their nineties, so whether that was due to good genes, hard work, or vegetarianism and Corn Flakes—who's to say?

Rumor has it that some Ohioans eat a frozen mousse featuring bleu cheese.

Culinary Firsts

With all of that ingenuity and all of that food, you have to expect that some of our most esteemed treats and novelties were introduced to America by clever Midwesterners. And it wasn't just the food but the preparation and service, too.

• • •

The ice cream sundae, which was a **great idea,** was born in a French-Canadian Settlement called Two Rivers, Wisconsin. Do you suppose the image of one river flowing into the next suggested the concoction?

Topeka, Kansas, was the site of the first Fred Harvey restaurant. Here's how that happened. Fred Harvey came to America from England and landed a job on the railroad in Chicago, Illinois. He was surprised by the poor quality of food available for passengers and eventually sought to remedy the situation by opening a restaurant at—yes—the depot in Topeka, Kansas. The Santa Fe line loved him and he opened more eateries. His restaurants were notable for their fine food, excellent service, **Irish linen, and Sheffield silver.** After a while, he added efficient and clean lodging, and Harvey Houses were born. He died in 1901, leaving forty-seven restaurants, thirty dining cars, and fifteen hotels.

The Eskimo Pie was patented in Onawa, Iowa, by C. K. Nelson in **a chilly January in 1922.** The delicious treats have been cooling us off ever since.

Wisconsin wanted to **differentiate their cheese** from everyone else's, so they began what's become a standard practice: color coding of cheese.

Kansans use left-over mashed potatoes in chocolate cake.

You Eat What?

Perhaps no one has commented more bluntly on our inventiveness (or gastric tolerance) than Ms. Emily Faithfull:

". . . The American stomach has been for years, generally and individually, the laboratory of the profoundest experiments in the matter of peculiar mixtures."
–EMILY FAITHFULL, 1884

What the heck is lutefisk anyway? Well, what you've heard is true. It's **cod soaked in lye.** That's the short version. And you have to soak out the lye (or *somebody* has to soak it out) before you eat it. Now, I know that sounds bad, but think of other things you eat—bleu cheese? (Viruses right there on your tongue, you know.) Corned beef? (I have no idea how that happens, but I know that meat directly from the cow is not corned.) Raw oysters? Need I say more?

Three surprising things that might make some people nostalgic: dandelion wine, buffalo—burgers or stew, **tomato soup cakes**. (Yes, tomato soup cake is distinct among cakes because of its pale red color and snappy flavor. I don't know who invented it, but it makes our friends at Campbell's happy.)

Amish friendship breads are distinguished by having a "starter" similar to sour dough. The yeast mixture is added to and **stirred and allowed to grow,** then a portion of it is used to make a fresh loaf of bread, and the process begins again.

A soup consisting of cheddar cheese, **sausage, and beer** can only be found in Wisconsin.

Kansas: first in wheat production, sorghum production, prairie chicken harvest.

Ice Cream

It was the double-dip ice cream cones and water fountains that "sold" me on the small town of Winchester, Indiana. Not that my feelings about the town mattered one whit, considering that my father had already accepted a promotion and had already rented a two-bedroom house for our family of seven! Within walking distance of that house though were the delights of the town square—courthouse solidly in the center, with each corner guarded by a piece of war memorabilia and sturdy hardwood trees providing shade to those who "hung out."

Thirty years ago, it was a safe place—both town and square; downtown streets provided a harmless place for young drivers to "cruise." The square was one-stop shopping at its best. The meat market, where I could count on a taste of the bologna or cheese my mother bought every week; Engle's Music Store; the Western Auto with its shiny bikes; the wooden-floored five-and-dime, with its distinctive and strange odors; one expensive clothing store, and one local J.C. Penney-type where my family shopped. And, of course, the drug stores—three, as I recall.

At twelve, I was most interested in those double-dip cones. The variety of flavors provided an agonizing decision. Two scoops of the same flavor or one each of chocolate and chocolate mint chip? And not, as one might suspect, one atop the other, but side by side! No more losing the top scoop and, more important to me—a person who eats one thing at a time, perfect for keeping the flavors separate.

Winchester, Indiana and I were going to be OK. Good ice cream took care of that.

Susan J. Barker
Bloomington, Indiana

Dinners in the Midwest have been the noon meal; suppers are at dusk.

Food as Ritual

Open the champagne, go out for sundaes, bring in the birthday cake. Food serves as ritual and punctuates celebrations, and sometimes food is the celebration to honor a job well done. This universal practice has some midwestern peculiarities. Of course. That's why this book exists.

• • •

A while back, the last day of school was a big celebration. Parents brought baskets of food, and the oldest girl student was assigned the honor of making the "stew," a concoction of **whiskey, water, sugar, allspice, and butter** to be served piping hot. Teachers who occasionally overindulged were said to be "stewed." Oh, so that's how it happened.

The ripening of corn marked the end of one year and the beginning of the next for Plains tribes. In many tribes no member would eat or handle any part of the harvest until after the **Festival of First Fruits.**

The Scottish called the New Year "Hogmanay" and celebrated by joining with friends to **drink ale and eat shortbread** and cakes and a special concoction called blackbun, which was a pastry filled with raisins and spices.

Food has often been "ritual" as much as it's been sustenance. Some tribes, before **going on the warpath,** would avoid all meat.

Kansas Indians prepared for war with a feast in the chief's tent, centered on roast dog. The tradition of eating an animal capable of sacrificing itself in order to save its master was similar to practices **all around the globe** at some stage of civilization. The partakers hoped, literally, to instill the same valiant characteristics in themselves.

Using up left-overs might mean green tomato pie.

There came a time in the Midwest when the crude sod houses and log cabins gave way to woodframe houses. This development, prevalent in the 1840s, was made possible partially by the arrival of more homesteaders, which meant there were more people to help with construction. The house- or barn-raisings took place on a single day, often in April, **when the weather was likely to be kind.** Settlers prepared by constructing a frame and assembling each of the four walls on the ground along each side of the foundation. When folks arrived—and often fifty to sixty-five families were invited—the men tipped the walls upright and secured them with crossbeams, joists, and braces. The roof—depending upon the type and how large it was—may also have been a project for that day or left to be taken care of later by the owners.

Once the work was completed, a giant meal was eaten. Women had cooked and baked all day, including bread on the Johnny- or Journey-cakes boards, which were about two feet long and eight inches wide. The dough was spread across the board, which was then leaned next to the fire. When one side was baked, the bread was flipped and the other side was cooked. After the food was eaten, men played sports—**arm-wrestling,** shooting, running races, and jumping. The custom of such raisings and the celebrations that accompanied them was abandoned around the turn of the century, when other construction methods became popular.

Pumpkin butter was another fall production. Sliced pumpkin was boiled, then strained, then boiled down. Sometimes it was **thickened with apples.** A delicious bread spread.

Our ancestors made pickles from watermelon rind, peaches, cabbage, and more.

In southern Illinois and in Minnesota, the French pleased the early tribespeople by serving two types of donuts. The batter was the same, but the *galette sauvages* were **oblong with three slits;** the *croquecignolles* were twice as large and slit several times. Other French food that was introduced early in America included crêpes and brioche (the sweet, rich dough was the critical element, rather than the double ball shape we associate with it now). Bouillon was a favorite drink of the French for such events as card parties; it was served with crackers or bread. It was still a popular drink in southern Illinois in the 1930s.

Scandinavians in southern Wisconsin liked to get together for lutefisk suppers. It was not uncommon for two thousand people to descend on a small church that had announced the event. Some Scandinavians were so possessive of their fish feasts that they expressed concern that too many "foreigners" were availing themselves of the treat. One editor wrote that the Germans and Irish were **"invading the sacred lutefisk domains"** and eating more than they should have. So much for the midwestern generosity.

One homesteaders' party took place at the **fall harvest of apples.** The event was called an "apple peeling."

The men were in charge of peeling. They sat in a circle around a stoneware jar, where they placed each peeled and quartered apple. Every man was given crock after crock of apples, and they kept track of how many they'd done, because the one who emptied the most crocks got to **kiss the woman of his choice.** After the work was done, the rug in the parlor was rolled back and everybody danced to the tunes of the local fiddler and other musicians.

The next day a few women returned to make apple butter. The peeled apples were steeped all day in a copper kettle outdoors and stirred with eighteen-foot-long ladles. Just as it was finishing, the **right amount of clove oil** was added. Ta-da.

Two ways to eat apple pie: a slice of cheddar cheese on top or in a bowl with milk.

Pitch-in or pot luck dinners after funerals were (and still are) common in many midwestern areas. In Indiana, neighbor women **cleared the house of all signs of death** and had the meal ready for mourners returning from the gravesite.

Pot lucks have had a strong history in Iowa, part of many occasions, including farm picnics, family reunions, all-day quilting bees, church or lodge socials, or other gatherings. A recent version of such things began in the mid-1970s and continued for more than a decade. Some faculty members from Cornell College and other folk in Mount Vernon, Iowa, began an **"eating collective"** that operated Monday through Thursday nights. Six to eight people ate together on each night, and some singles joined the group every one of the nights; others participated only one night per week. Cooking rotated so that all participants took turns. The rules were two: Dinner began at six and was over near half past seven so people could carry on with their evening activities; the cook never had to wash the dishes. Just another one of those community things. You could do this yourself.

Donation parties may have been the predecessor of fairs. The parties were often held to donate goods to the new minister, but homesteaders used them as an opportunity to **show off their best produce,** crops, pickles, canned fruits, hams, sausages, and other goods from their homes or root cellars.

The traditional **Polish Christmas meal** has nine courses—none of them meat. Fish is included in three of the courses, cheese and eggs are in two others, and vegetables and sweets comprise the rest.

Corncob jelly and corncob syrup: Waste not, want not.

The Ice Man Cometh

I watch my granddaughters hold their glasses under their automatic ice maker to get a cool drink, and my thoughts go back to the early 1930s and depression days in the Midwest. The endless hot days of summer were not easily relieved; we had no refrigerator.

If people wanted ice for their ice boxes, they hung a white card in their front window with the number of pounds that they needed—or could afford. The ice man slowly drove by in his flat-bed truck, looking for the signs telling him to stop.

We kids ran after him, and when he stopped and threw a chunk of ice up on his shoulder to take into a house, we climbed up on the back of his truck and looked for the small pieces of ice that broke away as he'd chipped the twenty-five or fifty-pound chunk.

It was wonderful—a cold, clear piece of ice to suck on—or cool our faces.

When the ice man returned to his truck, he never let on that he knew we'd hopped aboard. I wonder if he didn't leave those chunks just for us. We were grateful.

Teresa P. Costigan
Lansing, Michigan

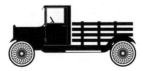

Cornmeal, among other things, is also a dip for okra.

Corn—A Celebration

Corn, indigenous to this hemisphere, was and continues to be the principal food in many cultures. In the Midwest, it is not only a staple—for people and cows, too—but a primary center of the agricultural success of the area. And yet, how much do you really know about those little yellow kernels? Not as much as you will in a few minutes.

Every strand of corn silk is connected to a **kernel of corn.**

Corn is the **oldest of cultivated plants,** older than wheat or rice.

Christopher Columbus was the first European to see and eat corn. He was so pleased that he—and other early explorers from Spain—took it back to Europe, along with its name, maize. Somewhere in the process of trade, the Anglo-Saxon word "Korn," which was **a general word for wheat** and small grains, was applied to the hardy, multi-colored nuggets, and "corn" is what stuck.

Corn probably first grew in the area that is Guatemala. **Peru** has also been considered the first site.

Native tribes along the East Coast did not have the rich soil that corn loves. They compensated by including a **protein-and-mineral-rich fish** in the mound of dirt into which a corn seed was planted.

Iowa is the number one corn producer. **Corn is in 1,200 different food items** and is part of more than 360 different products, including paint, batteries, mouthwash, and gasoline.

One-third of U.S. cranberries grow in Wisconsin.

Corn evolved from the flinty, tough, original ears into plumper, softer kernels through the efforts of farmers selecting and saving the best-looking ears for seed. One of the most successful early farmers was James L. Reid, an Ohioan, who moved to Illinois and fortuitously mixed "Gordon Hopkins" seed with "Little Yellow." His **accidental hybrid** was named "Reid's Yellow Dent" and was popular for quite a while. It had twice as many kernels as the native corn he'd begun with, and it won a lot of prizes.

Reid and his wife slept on their twenty best ears of corn—the ears were literally stored under the mattress—so the Reids didn't have to worry about the golden grains being lost or stolen. Jealous neighbors occasionally went into the fields at night and planted mongrel corn to mess things up. It caused temporary setbacks. Not all Midwesterners are the nicest and most unselfish people on the planet. We know that.

Seed-corn Gospel Trains originated in Iowa with a Michigan professor named Holden. The trains held a traveling exhibit and stopped at depots where farmers gathered round—the same way people would attend **chautauquas**—to hear the lectures and improve their crops.

Fallacies about the cornbelt. Tall corn. The record for tall corn goes to Lawrence Flander of Harper, Iowa. It was twenty-three feet and two-and-a-half-inches tall and it was exhibited as a sort of freak at **circuses and traveling shows.** But in fact no farmer wants corn that tall. It draws too much out of the soil and picking the corn would be more than a little tricky.

Truth or rumor? Yes, you can **listen to corn grow at night.** Try a night when it's a few feet high right after a dry spell followed by a good, long rain. In the right conditions, corn can grow eight inches in twenty-four hours. With that much activity, you're bound to hear something.

Indiana—fifth in the production of corn, but **first in popcorn.**

Nicknames for corn things: "Common-doin's" and "knick-knacks"—bread and pone.

Odd Facts

Kansans, early this century, made it against the law to eat various things in public. Included were **snakes, lizards, scorpions, and centipedes.** Thank you.

Almost thirty-five percent of Topeka, Kansas, citizens **eat their Oreos** by twisting them open.

By the way, Omaha consumes **less mayonnaise** than any city in the nation. The same wouldn't be said about Miracle Whip.

Some food wisdom from long ago shows how our attitudes have changed along with our knowledge. In the 1830s, newspapers and journals about health reported that fresh fruit and **vegetables were dangerous.** They were thought to be a potential source of cholera, and it was claimed that no one, whether gentleman farmer, woman or child, could gain health advantages by eating "vegetable matter which had not been softened or changed by culinary processes."

Campbell's chicken noodle is Cincinnati's favorite. **Indianapolis loves chili beef,** and St. Louis prefers New England clam chowder.

North Dakota insists that if **buttered popcorn** is advertised, the popcorn had better have butter on it. And that's just good sense.

Ohio is a state with an official state beverage—tomato juice. Here's why. Ohio **leads the country in production of tomato juice;** it's second to California in tomato production.

Do you suppose the publishers of *Midwest Living* are more flattered or more annoyed when it learns that **recipes have been torn** out of the library's copy of the magazine?

Of the major peanut butter brands, Jif is the biggest seller in the Midwest.

A Minneapolis City Council candidate was once **indicted for handing out Twinkies,** Ho-Hos, Kool-Aid and more to senior citizens. The thirty-four dollars worth of refreshments was probably seen as a bribe more than a health hazard.

Gary, Indiana, used to forbid its citizens to go to a theater after they'd eaten garlic. And in Waterloo, Nebraska, **barbers were not to eat onions** during working hours.

What do you suppose inspires people to name a town after food?
> **Sandwich,** Illinois
> **Rice,** Minnesota
> **Bismarck,** North Dakota

In southern Missouri, a tourist attraction of a rather unusual type draws customers hour after hour. Lambert's Cafe, with locations in both Sikeston and Branson, is home of the "throwed roll" restaurant. Begun in May 1976, the roll-throwing was an act of convenience for one eager customer, but enthusiasm for the shenanigans inspired the owner to keep throwing rolls, and that's what they do. The toss may be a few feet or across several tables, but if you give a nod (or even make eye contact!) to **the gentleman with the hot bun cart,** a fat roll will be pitched in your direction. The restaurant makes over two million of them annually and serves them up with molasses, butter, fried okra, and numerous other luscious temptations of down-home cooking.

Chicken was called the **"gospel bird"** in southern Illinois and southern Indiana, because it was served when the preacher came to visit.

Candy cigarettes were once illegal in North Dakota.

Free-range pigs? Cincinnati's pig population in the 1850s was described by many travelers. The **porkers lounged in the gutters** and strolled down the street with the same freedom as birds or squirrels enjoy today. They were of course useful in controlling garbage, but they were also known to bump into people occasionally, their portly bodies knocking down the unsuspecting tourist. I presume that despite their sweet freedom, they were occasionally butchered and eaten.

Mentone, Indiana, population not quite one thousand, salutes its egg industry with the display of a **three-thousand-pound egg.** There's no information available about the chicken that laid it.

To satisfy a desire for fruits after a long winter when it was still too early for any such thing in the larder, housewives invented **vinegar pie.** The tart and sweet custard of vinegar, molasses, water, and nutmeg offered some satisfaction until ripe fruits were available. I have to say that this is a prime example of keeping the cheery side out.

The Top Ten Ingredients for Jell-O:

10. Spam
9. Chicken noodle soup
8. Cottage cheese
7. Sliced bananas
6. Nuts, preferably walnuts
5. Whipped cream
4. Grated carrots
3. Pineapple
2. Fruit cocktail
1. **Marshmallows**

Thirty-five percent of all cheese consumed in the U.S. is made in Wisconsin.

How We Have Fun

Fun is a good thing but only when it spoils nothing better.

– George Santayana (1863–1952)

Midwesterners know how to enjoy each other and how to have a good time. It doesn't always come naturally, but they get better each year. As their ancestors arrived in the middle of America, they celebrated with the religious, seasonal, and family events that they had brought with them from wherever they came. As time passed, people found more to value and consequently, more to celebrate. When, for instance, weeks passed on the prairie with no visitors to the homestead, the arrival of a passer-by became a reason for at least a small celebration.

And the hard work necessary for survival often led to celebrations. People didn't raise a barn and go home. They ate, as you read in "Our Wonderful Food," and if it wasn't against their religion, they danced. Big jobs, such as making a season's worth of soap or peeling and coring a harvest of apples, called for help. Farmers gathered at one home at a time and helped each other do the work. And then they ate, played sports, danced, and enjoyed each other's company.

It wasn't long before the tasks of farming developed into show-cases, contests, and competitions. County fairs and friendly "meets"

143

offered opportunities to display prize produce and compete at the skills of farming, like corn husking.

Some of these activities are still part of our celebrations—county and state fairs with competitions for everything from pies and tomatoes to talent fests. We may not chase greased pigs as often, but plenty of porkers are roasted whole and eaten every summer. There may no longer be wagon races down main streets, but instead you can witness a "tractor pull." (And what, my West Coast friend asks, is a tractor pull? A tractor with a large, flat platform attached behind it moves forward as long as it can while more and more weight—sometimes even parade watchers who hop on—is added. Eventually, the tractor, belching smoke and with wheels spinning, reaches its limit and is stopped in its tracks. OK? *A tractor pulls,* so it's called a tractor pull.) For those who miss bygone activities, such as the threshing of wheat by old-fashioned machines, there are plenty of demonstrations of how it used to be done "in the old days."

We celebrate our varied heritage in another way across the Midwest, with town "days" that honor the founding ethnic group or a particular aspect of the community. If it's not Finn Days or Swede Days, it might be Bratwurst or Beet Days. These two- or three-day festivals showcase quilts, roses, mums, tulips, antique cars, trains, and jazz, bluegrass, and blues music and more. They feature parades, balloon ascensions, and kite-flying, and they sponsor sports of all kinds from skiing to road races.

When these "days" focus on heritage, citizens celebrate the cultural traditions that were part of the early community—the costumes, the dances, and the music. And don't forget the food. Celebrating a town's history in such vivid ways deepens the sense of community for people of all generations.

Towns also celebrate their economic foundation—Monroe, Wisconsin, brings you Cheese Days—and their midwestern sense of humor—Minneota, Minnesota, celebrates its boxelder bugs. Why not? A city in Michigan uses winter weather to build an ice palace in the center of town, while an Iowa town holds a January golf tournament. Such mid-winter fun is not such a far reach from the inventiveness of the earlier Midwesterners—give them lemons and they make lemonade.

The thing is this: In the Midwest, we have not just fifty-two weekends per year, we have fifty-two per state, which is 624. And in a broader sense we don't have just 624 weekends, we have (approximately) 62,556 weekends among all the counties we have in the Midwest. That's a lot of Saturdays and Sundays to fill. Who can blame us for our celebrations—the large as well as the small?

Midwesterners find scores of other ways to have fun beyond festivals. We ski, we skate, we golf, we swim, we ride bikes. We do it alone or with friends. Sometimes, as in The *Des Moines Register*'s Annual Great Bike Ride Across Iowa, RAGBRAI, we do it with 10,000 friends. Or we revel in a weekend full of a community-wide version of Trivial Pursuit as in Appleton, Wisconsin every spring. And we put on plays and musicals and operas, and as always we go to see touring shows of all kinds. Once it was Chautauqua, now it's speeches by Nobel Prize winners or music at Lollapalooza.

What follows is a slim sampling of how Midwesterners have fun. There was lots to choose from—books full of it. Been there, done that? Well, you can *always* find more. In fact, you could start a brand new festival—honoring, well, you'll think of something.

Taking Ourselves Seriously (Not)

Who would imagine that someone would think it was a fun thing to wear molded plastic cheese on his or her head? Well, people got fed up with being called "Cheeseheads," and T.J. and Michelle Peterslie of Onalaska, Wisconsin, decided to do something about it. They "invented" Cheddar-heads, those giant plastic hats that are now worn with pride and a golden, cheddar glow. They sell like, well, about as well as cheese in Wisconsin, which is a mighty amount.

An added attraction is that they can save your life. Did you hear about the fan who was in a private plane accident a while back, and he had a cheesehead on his lap. The "cushion" apparently kept him from being seriously injured. You just never know.

• • •

Sheboygan, Wisconsin's July 4 festivities include the Great Cardboard Boat Regatta, a race in which people **don't waste time loitering** while their boats sit in the water.

Iowa has a weird little thing on July 4, too. It's the annual parade in Cedar Bluff where anybody can enter anything. **Sounds innocent enough.** A continuing theme of many entries over the years has been carp (the fish not the whiney yapping, though plays-on-words are part of the fun), for some reason, and the "floats," which have been lovingly thrown together the night before the parade, often skewer politicians and news events from the previous year. Some of the non-carp highlights have been the "Briefcase Marching Band" and the "Statue of Liberty Gals," who marched bare-breasted, which raised a fuss.

Dale Smith of Tipp City, Ohio, invented the "fuzz buster" radar detector.

Garretson, South Dakota, celebrates their Belgian past with a little-known sport (outside of Garretson) called Roly-Boly. Roly-Boly is a bit like horseshoes except that the "horseshoes" are round wooden discs weighted on one side. The object of the game is to see how close to the peg the player can put his wooden disc. **A lot of Belgian jokes** get tossed along with the roly-bolys. (What's a Belgian joke?)

Barn Dance

Each Saturday night in the early 1930s, the Pavelka family (yes, from Willa Cather's *My Antonia*) hosted a barn dance for teenagers. The eldest sons of the family chaperoned the gathering. Discipline was strict but it was almost unnecessary, since most of us felt privileged to be there.

We were invited up the steps to the loft, lighted by lanterns, where benches lined the walls. Music was provided by an old hand-cranked record player. Teenagers from towns around Webster County mingled, danced, and became acquainted. I met my future husband the summer of 1932.

After fifty years of marriage we drove back to the deserted farmstead to visit that old barn again. It seemed smaller somehow but it was all there—the barn, trees, and memories of our friends— and that lady in the rocker under the tree. She was and always will be "My Antonia," too.

LaVona Armstrong Borwege
Blue Hill, Nebraska

More coal is shipped out of Toledo, Ohio, than anywhere in the nation.

Some Sports Bits

The **first major league All-Star Game** was held at Comiskey Park in Chicago, Illinois, on July 6, 1933.

"**L**et's win one for the Gipper." Ronald Reagan? Knute Rockne? No. George Gipp. Gipp was a player for Rockne, who died while he was a college student playing football for the famous coach. Winning **one for the Gipper** became a standard urging from Rockne to his players. Knute Rockne, born in 1888 to a Norwegian carriage maker, coached for Notre Dame after being a student there and then a chemistry instructor. In thirteen years, the team lost only twelve games and never a season.

Walter Perry Johnson, Humboldt, Kansas, was one of the first five men chosen to be in the Hall of Fame when, in 1936, the National Baseball Hall of Fame opened. His 1913 record of pitching fifty-six consecutive scoreless innings stood until 1968. Johnson's nickname was "Big Train" on behalf of his chief weapon—**a mean fast ball** considered to be the fastest at that time.

David Scott Collins, born in 1952 in Rapid City, South Dakota, is also known for speed on the baseball field. He **stole seventy-nine bases** with the 1980 Cincinnati Reds and sixty bases when he was with the 1984 Toronto Bluejays. Maybe he took the name of his birthplace very seriously.

A player who used an unusual offense was "Biter" Jones from Washington University in St. Louis, Missouri. He had an undershot jaw and he was famous for biting his enemies. Over time, he **bit eleven guards,** two centers and a flankerback, but he only lost sixty-five yards to penalties. His coach, Jim Cozelman, said that not only did he not mind that "Biter" used his teeth from time to time, but, in fact, Jones was one of the finest guards he'd ever coached.

In 1929, in Ohio, iron and steel were the leading industries.

The football huddle was introduced by a coach nicknamed "Little Dutchman," when he coached at the University of Illinois. Coach Robert Zuppke was **German-born and Wisconsin-raised.**

Sparky (George Lee) Anderson, born in Bridgewater, South Dakota, was the **first manager to win the World Series in both the National and American Leagues.** He lead the Cincinnati Reds to two World Series, four pennants and five division titles in nine years and he lead the Detroit Tigers to two division titles in the 1984 World Series.

Leo Schlick of St. Viator College in Indiana had **a fabulous afternoon in 1916,** scoring one hundred points, including twelve touchdowns. Bad day for the other team.

Bobby Knight, born in 1940 in **Massilon, Ohio**. Little did his parents imagine the chaos and inspiration he would cause.

And now a word from one of our own . . .

What I miss most about the Midwest:

- simple square blocks with north-south and east-west streets
- automobiles (seemingly) without horns
- commercial employees who smile and call you by name
- neighborhoods without real or imagined fences
- homes without alarm systems
- hands without middle fingers

— ROBERT E. ALLEN, CEO, AT&T

Wisconsin forbids the manufacture of cigars in a basement.

Hooping in the Hayloft

Barn ball was big in Indiana when I was growing up. Our barn was the hot spot on Saturday and Sunday afternoons if you were looking for a good pick-up game. We had the advantage of having not one basketball hoop in our hayloft, but *two*, for exciting, full-court action. Our court came with a half-court line formed by the birds roosting above.

I would faithfully watch the games every weekend afternoon, perched up high on the bales of hay, dreaming of the day when I would be old enough to play with the big kids. I had two older sisters in high school who played—no doubt another attraction for the boys to come to our barn to play. I don't think my sisters were too terribly excited to have their little ten-year-old sister tagging along to the games, but I never missed one. I saw players slam dunk with the aid of a barn beam sticking out in just the right place. They seemed to fly through the air.

I practiced in the barn almost daily, pretending to be Ann Myers of UCLA. I never left the barn without making ten free throws in a row.

One day, to my astonishment, my hard work paid off. I was sitting in my usual spot when Steve Stickel, the best player and organizer of the games (on whom I had a big crush), looked up at me and asked me to play. My heart was thumping as I scrambled off the bales and onto the court. The game began and they treated me as an equal, passing me the ball and encouraging me to shoot it. And shoot it I did! I don't recall missing one shot the whole game. What a thrill for me to hear the seasoned teenaged players give me compliments about my playing. That was the first of many barn ball games to come.

Debra Brownsberger-Keyes
Oak Park, Illinois

Arthur McArthur, Sr., was governor of Wisconsin for three days in 1856.

Stars

There are all manner of stars—movie, television, music, and the arts. Sports is full of them, too. Here's a tiny sampling of Midwesterners who have watched their stars rise as they held, batted, or threw a ball properly or rode a horse in a designated fashion. If only it were so simple.

• • •

Tennis star Jimmy Connors was born in East St. Louis, Illinois. He won many national titles, **the U.S. Open Singles Championship five times,** and the 1982 Wimbledon title.

John Heisman, who played and coached football in the late 1800s and early 1900s, is buried in Rhinelander, Wisconsin. The Heisman Trophy's namesake invented and devised many plays, including **the center snap,** the forward pass, and he initiated the use of the word "hike" to begin a play.

Of course an Indiana native would be the first basketball player to score more than three thousand points in a season. **Wilt Chamberlain** of Fort Wayne, Indiana, scored a total 3,033 points by March 10, 1961.

Elroy "Crazy Legs" Hirsch, born in 1923 in Wausau, Wisconsin, said he gained the unusual nickname because as a kid he used to practice dodging around the trees near his home. His ability won him both **popularity and fame.** Ironically, with all that agility, he had many injuries; once he had to stop playing for an entire year to heal a skull fracture. In 1951 Hirsch had the most receptions, receiving yardage, average yards per receptions, and touchdown receptions for the whole NFL. Wow.

Illinoisan Seth Barnes Nicholson discovered the 9th, 10th, and 11th moons of Jupiter.

Burl Sane (1898–1968) was born in Groton, South Dakota, and became a jockey with the colorful nicknames "The Dutchman" and "Handy Guy." He won 968 races, riding such famous horses as Man o' War and Gallant Fox, with whom he won the Triple Crown in 1930. He's considered by some to be **the greatest jockey in history.**

Casey Tibbs (1929–1990) was a world champion saddle bronc rider, who was named "all-around champ" by the **Professional Rodeo Cowboys Association** in 1951. You might remember his appearance on the cover of *Life* magazine that year.

Vince Lombardi had been a head coach only at the high school level when he came to Green Bay, Wisconsin, to coach the Packers. He had assisted at West Point and with the New York Giants, but in Wisconsin, **he took charge,** and the team, which he rearranged, turned around, and took to the Super Bowl twice, won five league titles. The Packers included Bart Starr, Jim Taylor, Ray Nitschke, and Paul Hornung. Lombardi owed a lot to the players and the players owed a lot to him. Starr and Nitschke both ended up in the Pro-Football Hall of Fame.

Otto Graham, from Waukegan, Illinois, is the only person to be named a college **All-American** in both football and basketball. He was a College All-Star in 1943 and went on to play for the Cleveland Browns of the new All-America Football Conference.

South Dakota has more than 73,000 miles of road, including 80% paved.

Free Shows

In the mid-1950s, several times a month, on a Saturday night during summertime, a roving movie showman would come to town. He drove into town with his equipment packed into a trailer that he pulled behind his car. He brought his own projector and speakers, a huge movie screen (about ten feet by ten feet), and, of course, the movies.

The town had a vacant, grassy lot on main street; this lot became the outdoor "movie theater." Because the town held the "free shows" regularly, permanent wooden poles were erected near the back side of the open lot to support the movie screen. The town lumber yard brought cement blocks and planks and set up bleachers. Some folks brought blankets or lawn chairs to sit on. Others would sit in their cars.

People came from our town, and from surrounding towns and farms to watch the movies. The town's businesses sponsored the monthly movies as a way of increasing local revenue, and it worked. The "free shows" brought lots of people into town, and they often came early to conduct their business before the show started. Naturally, there were many refreshments sold before, during, and after the show as well.

I liked those Saturday nights because I could see my school friends who lived outside of town, and I was always given a nickel or a dime to indulge in some candy. The movie subjects varied from week to week. I recall not liking the romantic "kissing and hugging" stuff at that age, but I thoroughly enjoyed the "Ma and Pa Kettle" series. The occasional color cartoon was also a thrill.

These "giant" outdoor movies were a big treat, an important way we had fun when we were growing up.

Linda Walkner Knell
Council Bluffs, Iowa

Ohio's first capital was Chillicothe.

Hog-Calling

If you live in the Midwest, it's likely that you had a relative who called hogs. (Just ask around—somebody will admit to it.) Hog-calling started because people didn't have fences and if the hogs didn't come to eat, they went hungry, and the farmers lost potential income or food. Hog-calling grew to something of an art, and even after fences were built, people still called hogs. Neighbors competed against each other, and eventually it became a standard part of county fairs and state fairs and even national championships, the first of which was in 1924.

Fred Patzel of Madison, Nebraska, was one of the first men who was truly championship material. In 1926, he was invited to radio station WJAG to do his famous hog call over the radio. His performance was so effective that he blasted a tube; the radio had to go off the air. Afterwards, he commented that he wondered what would have happened if he hadn't restrained himself. There was no report on how many hogs came running.

And here's a tale about a hog-calling contest held in July 1926, in Des Moines, Iowa. At that time, judges had five criteria to look for in hog-calling. One, of course, was carrying quality, so the call had to be loud. But second on the list was hog appeal since hogs were the things that needed to listen up. Variety was third; apparently the hogs liked that. Fourth was musical appeal, whatever that may have been. And, finally, distinctness, so that the hogs wouldn't be confused about who was calling, I guess.

The contest in Des Moines was a little unusual because of its distinguished judges. One of them, not surprisingly, was the editor of the farm magazine, *Wallace's Farmer.* He was the uncle of Henry A. Wallace,

Chester Gould's anger at Al Capone led to the invention of Dick Tracy in 1931.

and his name was John Wallace. But another judge happened to be John Philip Sousa, who must have been visiting the area at the time for perhaps another musical occasion. When the forty-seven contestants lined up, Sousa leaned over to the judge next to him and said, "I thought that we were supposed to be judging the hogs, not the people." Well, there was a few moments of awkwardness and the rules were explained to the *maestro* and things proceeded.

The winner was a person named Milford Beeghly from Pierson, Iowa, and he explained that his winning hoot was successful partly because he breathed three times instead of twice. He started with a "who-ee." He repeated it at a different, higher pitch, then he breathed twice and went into the "piggy" which was first "*Pig*-ee" and then, "Pig-*eeee*," getting higher all the time and ending with a trill. He said he didn't know why, but for some reason the hogs and judges always liked the trill.

In his later years, Beeghly owned seventy hogs whereas he once had had five hundred. But every once in a while, he'd let out with a call. The hogs would lift their snouts, flap their ears, and listen, but times change, and they didn't know what all the fuss was about. By then, hogs were on self-feeders and could chow down whenever they wanted to. But that's no reason not to step outside and try the old one-two-three once in a while. Go for it.

More than 425 species of birds are seen in Kansas—from tiny hummingbirds to bald eagles.

Winter Won't Stop Us

There is a part of each Midwesterner that cheers when the weather station shows Minnesotans struggling through blustery January mornings to walk the thirty-foot gauntlet from bus to office door. "Yeah, hang in there!" we're thinking. We know we're a little nuts to live in such a climate, but it makes us feel tough. And many of us have found ways to flaunt our pride. How? We have fun. You're invited to join in.

● ● ●

Curling came to the United States with the Scots in 1855. It's very popular in Wisconsin, with over thirty clubs and **more than four thousand curlers.**

For those of you feeling that late-winter, couch-potato thing at the end of February, roll out to your car and drive to Auxvasse, Missouri, or if you're feeling really lazy, have a friend drive you. It's **Loafers' Week.** Each morning, you can go to the community hall, play cards, gossip, and have the daily lunch of home-cooked favorites. There are peanuts to eat and you can exercise your lethargy by dropping the shells on the floor. Afternoon is more of the same.

The Norwegian Birkebiner is a race that commemorates the rescue, almost eight hundred years ago, of **Norway's infant king** by two soldiers on skis. Each year the route is retraced over a mountain path in Norway. The American Birkebiner is held in Haward, Wisconsin, in honor of the Norwegian version.

For the truly hardy, the **John Beargrease** Sled Dog Marathon in Duluth, Minnesota, has thirty teams from across North America who mush the five hundred miles from Duluth to Grand Portage and back.

Chicago is the third largest city in the country with a population over 2,700,000.

Softball was begun by a reporter for the Chicago Board of Trade in 1887. George Hancock didn't want to be **without baseball** all winter. Softball was his indoor alternative.

Some Midwesterners defy the winter weather by taking on unusual challenges. At Crystal Lake, Illinois, the Chili Open Golf Classic invites players to "drive, putt and slide their way around two nine-hole courses." Other winter golf havens include Grand Haven and Spring Lake, Michigan, Port Clinton, Ohio, and Des Moines, Iowa, which sort of cheats—its winter golf game takes place entirely in the city's skywalk system. A few hours to the east, **hardier Iowans** in Cedar Rapids actually go outside for "polar bear" bike riding. Isn't it all just too much fun?

Falling into the "truly brave" category are those Midwesterners who, by bet or by some inclination that grows out of "old-country" healthful living, insist on swimming outdoors in the winter. And we're not talking hot tubs here. You can witness or join locals for a "polar bear" dip into some bracing ice water in several towns including Houghton, Michigan, and Sheboygan, Wisconsin (a town that also indulges in ice-bowling). In Mansfield, Ohio, exposure is taken to another height (or depth) as **bikini-clad skiers** race down slopes at their Winter Ski Carnival. And, finally, the "Ice Box of the Nation," International Falls, celebrates its revered title with a holiday that includes the Freeze Your Gizzard Blizzard Run. Now, are we going to see you all racing to the Midwest next winter?

The 1993 floods in the Midwest affected 9 states.

Ice Fishing

No DISCUSSION OF MIDWESTERN winter fun is complete without taking note of ice fishing, which is actually a useful sport, since like all fishing, it fetches dinner. Participants also seem to get a little extra kick out of the "homestead" feel.

Many Midwesterners go ice fishing every winter weekend, and they have "permanent" homes (most are about ten by sixteen feet) that stay on the ice for months. Leech Lake, near Walker, Minnesota, is filled with ice fishing houses, and rumor has it that some are three stories high and have hot tubs. Brainerd, Minnesota, has a special weekend devoted to the sport that draws five thousand people. That's a lot of little holes in the ice.

J.R. and Karen Peterson of Plymouth, Minnesota, have an ice house that includes bunk beds, stereo, and CD player. Theirs is one of about five thousand that sits on Mille Lacs in Minnesota. J.R. rigged an alarm system so that their four fishing holes can be active around the clock; if there's a nibble they'll be wakened. Their home received the top prize of 2,500 dollars in the 1996 Windsor Canadian Liquor's "Ultimate Ice House" contest. There's a Midwest contest for you.

In 1844 Nauvoo was Illinois' largest city.

Circus Notes from a Place or Two

Peru, Indiana, is a town with circus down to its marrow. Livery owner Ben Wallace and James Anderson started the Hagenbeck-Wallace Circus in the late 1880s, and Peru subsequently became a popular off-season home for many circuses. Clyde Beaty, whose name is practically synonymous with "circus," was a native of Peru.

Peru celebrates its heritage for a week in July with the usual parades and circus performances, but it's not your usual arrive-in-lots-of-trucks circus. The performers are drawn from the surrounding area and range in age from small children to people over eighty or even ninety. The requirement is that they must be residents of Miami County; many are descendants of earlier performers.

• • •

Baraboo, Wisconsin, a town of less than 10,000, preserves **a magical link with childhood.** Five sons of a German harnessmaker (about whom you've read elsewhere) presented a show in 1882 called "Classic and Comic Concert Company." The production eventually became the Ringling Brothers' Barnum and Bailey Circus, which used Baraboo as a home base until 1918. This local cultural icon is maintained by the Circus World Museum. Five big-top performances are given throughout the summer and there are *daily* circus parades.

Daily! Now *that* might make you feel like you're caught with Bill Murray—in your own "Ground Hog Day."

Finally, Delavan, Wisconsin, is home to the **Clown Hall of Fame and Research Center.** Ponder the questions—how large a shoe can a person wear and still walk? How much force can a cannon use to launch a clown into a net without causing serious injury? How much water can you carry in an artificial flower?

After Mormon leader Joseph Smith was murdered, most of Nauvoo moved west.

Weird Stuff

The next time you have a hamburger, think about Seamore, Wisconsin, where it all started. During Seamore Days **a meatball vendor** named Charlie Magreen was having a hard time selling his meatballs, so he flattened them and put them between bread and they started selling like, well, like burgers. The town also holds a record in the Guinness Book of World Records for the largest hamburger. The 1989 feat was accomplished with a 5,520 pound burger, and I don't know how many cows that would be—two or three, I suppose.

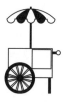

And what do some Midwesterners truly like to do for fun? Shop! I suppose it's the old hunting-and-gathering urge transferred from the great outdoors to the racks and racks of merchandise. And where do Midwesterners like to shop? Many places, but there's no place like the Mall of America. Tucked next door to the Minneapolis airport, the mall covers 4,200,000 square feet, and, contains an amusement park, miniature golf, 350 stores, and forty restaurants. The 13,000 parking spaces are often filled to the brim. What I'd like to know is if there's a **"nip 'n' nap,"** where you can have a little glass of sherry and rent a cot for thirty minutes. Has anybody invented that yet? Perhaps it's not necessary. A few years ago, statisticians figured out that people typically spent eighty-four dollars during a 2.6-hour visit. That amount of time would preclude a nap, though a nap might double shopping time. Entrepreneurs? Are you paying attention?

Chicago is third densest city in the nation for people per square mile: 12,252.

How about a glorious celebration of waste-not, want-not, a shop-till-you-drop, **eighty-five-mile-long garage sale.** Along the Minnesota/Wisconsin line in early May, people literally line up to sell their books, their dishes, their portable goods from Frontunac to Kellogg, Minnesota, and across the road, Ulma to Bay City, Wisconsin. Another use for a "nip 'n' nap," which of course you could find at your local tavern and hotel. Yes?

In Springfield, Illinois, it is illegal to toss dwarves in bars, even if they **wear padded suits.** It doesn't seem like a nice way to have fun.

Midwesterners, like people all over the country, love to collect. Fennimore, in Grant County, Wisconsin, has a museum with over five thousand dolls. The owner, Darlene Mueller, has been collecting for almost thirty years and she has **the largest Barbie collection** in the Midwest. In fact there's a Barbie room.

International Falls, Minnesota, must have had **a good excuse** to outlaw the chasing of dogs up telephone poles by cats. (Sorry, I don't always have the whole story on things—just the punch line.)

And if you want to sink into a big meat sandwich, one of the primo choices is Mayslack's Polka Bar in St. Paul, Minnesota. Before his death, Mayslack, **a former wrestler,** used to serve up the "best beef sandwiches in the world." The restaurant carries on the tradition, and packs in the customers. Though still tasty, it may not be quite as much fun since Mayslack was such a flirt. He apparently enjoyed tweaking the ladies' thumbs with his tongs. I know it sounds strange, but I guess it was fun.

Ohio has no natural lakes; they're all man-made.

The Sport of Octo-toss

THERE MUST BE SOMETHING about an ice arena that invites odd and assorted missiles. When hockey returned to popularity at the University of Wisconsin at Madison, fans waved and threw rubber chickens onto the rink, all the time yelling "Sieve!" The custom abated as officials got firm.

But what about Detroit. There, the Red Wings fans throw octopuses (octopi, if you love your Latin), and they're not even rubber. In fact, the standard preparation is twenty minutes on a hard boil with a little lemon and white wine to cut the odor. They say a well-cooked octopus can be hurled one hundred feet. This odd custom was begun during the playoffs in 1952 by former fishmonger Peter Cusimano. The team was going for its eighth straight win, and octopus appendages seemed like the logical good-luck charm. A perfectly decent, though perhaps foolhardy, connection. Throwers have refined the art of smuggling the dead creatures into the arena, and they study the methods of throwing, in order to have the entire corpse land on the ice rather than fall apart on unsuspecting fans during the wind-up. I don't know. If I were attending a Red Wings game, I'd be sure to look around at my immediate neighbors and take a few long whiffs to make sure I was in a seafood-free zone.

The largest cement plant in the country is in Alpena, Michigan.

Fun in the Old Days

I know what you're thinking. You're thinking, "Fun? This was all there was for fun?" Well, you might recall the piece on barn dances or the food and festivities after a barn-raising. Or what about corn-husking and hog-calling events. Put things in perspective. When people came to the Midwest, they came to work. This was not an invitation to Club Med, or Club Mid, as it were. We're talking here about back-breaking, sod-busting, build-your-own-house work. That's what they expected. A little newspaper reading was their idea of fun. Get the picture? OK.

• • •

Newton, Kansas, was a huge mecca for gamblers in the 1880s. Eight gambling halls were ready to entertain and have their coffers filled by **eager cowboys.**

In early corn-husking contests, lucky was the fellow who came across a red ear of corn: He got to **kiss his favorite girl.**

The **champion corn-husker** was Irvin Bauman from Illinois who could peel off 46.71 bushels in the allotted time. Steam-and-gas-powered machinery raised the capacity to one thousand bushels a day, and corn-husking contests faded away.

Jule-bokking was a Norwegian notion of fun. (No sneers.) Adults, or in some areas, children, dressed in full costume and went from house to house at Christmas time—often Christmas Eve. (I know it sounds like Halloween, but these are Norwegians we're talking about, and **sometimes they behave oddly.**) They acted silly or frightening, and sometimes they performed songs or gave recitations. If the hosts weren't teetotalers, there was a little drink as a reward for adults and cookies for children. Yes, it was fun.

Black River Falls, Wisconsin, is a former logging camp.

Abraham Lincoln was an active player in recreational activities in New Salem, Illinois. He showed off his strength by lifting a **barrel of whiskey** and drinking out of the tap hole.

Touring amusements that you may have witnessed in the larger cities in the 1800s included exhibitions of ventriloquism, a kaleidoscope, a mummy, glass-blowing; animals such as a giraffe, **elephant or ibex;** and human oddities, such as Siamese twins, a giant, Tom Thumb, Jr. (who was twenty-five inches tall), and people born without hands who performed various tasks with their toes. While many of these curiosities arrived from Europe and Africa, the American Midwest offered oddities for their Eastern friends—the buffalo and a large fish called a tunny.

And now, a word from our past . . .

The alarmingly pessimistic view of the bicycle question is not justified by facts. It is doubtless true that many young women ride to excess. It is also doubtless true that to the woman of impure life the wheel may offer a convenient means for facilitating the execution of immoral designs, but that the pastime itself has a tendency to degrade or demoralize is a proposition too absurd for a moment's consideration. A woman who will violate the decencies and proprieties of life while wheeling will violate them on other occasions. Where one woman rides to destruction on the wheel a thousand maintain all the deco-rum, modesty, and circumspection that characterize the well-bred, self-respecting women from the ideal American homes.

–THE CHICAGO TIMES HERALD, 1896

(Will people ever stop blaming technology for human downfall? Probably not.)

An immigrant might expect to earn $100 a year in the United States in 1845.

Good Clean Fun

It's not always easy for Midwesterners to indulge themselves. These are the people, you recall, who are still saving string and washing their aluminum foil and plastic bags. To blow a wad of money on delectable food, attentive service, or extravagant surroundings goes against the grain a little, and it takes some rationalizing to let it happen. But happen it does. On occasion.

● ● ●

Kenosha, Wisconsin, is home of the international headquarters for the Society for the Preservation of Barbershop Quartets. So you might expect to see more **red-and-white striped shirts** on their streets, along with men adorned by handlebar mustaches.

Roller skating was introduced in 1863 and grew wildly popular very quickly. Parents worried about the **safety of their children,** and employers worried about workers arriving at work exhausted from their long evenings of skating.

Becoming an Outdoors-Woman (BOW) **teaches women to shoot, hunt, fish, canoe, and use a chain-saw**. The workshop was begun by Christine Thomas and operates out of the College of Natural Resources at the University of Wisconsin-Stevens Point. (I've not yet located a group called BIM—Becoming an Indoors-Man, where men learn the finer points of clothing repair, dusting, pot-scrubbing, and how to use a vacuum. Sorry, guys. You know it's hard to resist these moments.)

Prairie root systems have been known to extend to a depth of 15 feet.

Norma (Duffy) Lyon has been carving a butter cow (yes, life-sized) and other subjects, including a Clydesdale horse, **Dwight and Mamie Eisenhower,** and Garth Brooks, for the Iowa State Fair for thirty-seven years. Her 1996 feat was the *American Gothic* in butter, as featured on the cover of this book.

In northeastern Iowa, life imitates art, sort of, at a **Field of Dreams Festival** in Dyersville, in early September. Baseball fans gather where Kevin Costner's movie, *Field of Dreams,* was filmed to play pick-up games or just toss a ball back and forth. Occasionally Headliner Charity Games have been held, featuring stars such as Reggie Jackson and Lou Brock.

Speaking of polka—and in the Midwest, there has always been someone who has just said the word "polka"—the dance is big around here because it's an unpretentious activity that requires dancers to be relaxed, uninhibited, and willing to breathe hard. All midwestern qualities.

The "dance with the skip in the middle" grew popular in central Europe as a **counterpoint to formal dances,** such as the minuet. And you can't get too serious when you dance to music coming from an accordion. Czechs and Germans brought it to America, and it persists with a vengeance. A joyful robust glee.

(I like to ponder how different native Omaha, Nebraskan Marlon Brando's movie *Last Tango in Paris* would have been if it had been instead *Last Polka in Minot* [North Dakota, you geography nuts]. We've got a whole new movie, and it's probably not rated X.)

What's thirty-two feet long, twelve feet across, bumpy, and yellow? Yes, a cob of corn. A big cob of corn. It was created by Dale Ungerer who assembled the amazing object with **1,700 plastic milk jugs,** paint, some wire, and an old grain augur. Ungerer, a truck driver by trade, will transport the cob around the Midwest for display at various events. Having a party? Give Dale a call.

Iowa has 5 times as many hogs as people.

Rope jumping—as a national "sport"—grew popular after Wally Mohrman, of Blumer, Wisconsin, Public Schools, decided to add a little competitive spice. The students weren't very interested, so he organized a contest. Ninety students out of nine hundred in the system competed in the finals of the first contest, and Blumer became the **Rope Jump Capital** of the world. Johnny Carson invited some Blumer Jumpers to appear on the Tonight Show and the contest spread. Now there are 10,000 jumpers competing nationally every year.

Wisconsin is a state of bicyclists. One of their favorite gatherings is the Chequamegon **Fat Tire Festival** held in Cable every year. Cable must be quite the fun-loving community (population eight hundred). The residents oversee a vacationing area that contains 150 lakes. Now that's fun.

Unlike New Glarus, Wisconsin, Minnesota will never have a full-blown William Tell festival. It's illegal there to aim arrows or other such pointed objects at **a target mounted on a person**. (And actually they don't *shoot* arrows at small children in New Glarus either, but they make it *look* as if they're doing so during the annual play about the big event. Apple on boy's head; you know the story.)

Windie—a tall tale designed either to impress or frighten newcomers to the West.

Throwing the Dishes In

After dinner, when we went to the lake, my father always threw the dishes over the boathouse deck. Family, guests, and a crowd of kids—my cousins—sat around on split log benches, awash in the light of the setting sun, stuffed and sticky with watermelon that had been kept cool in the spring all day. The lake below was as flat as a plate and sparkled with the sunset. We were quiet and happy; that day we already would have ridden our imaginary horses on the gravel road, visited fairy land, given a tea party with a clam shell tea service, transformed our beach towels into the gowns of princesses, swum to the raft, swamped the canoe, and feasted on sunshine until we were so full of it we glowed.

And then Dad announced, "Time to wash the dishes, Momma," and he'd send a plate spinning, frisbee style, out over the deck railing and we'd all feel our hearts go up our throats and part way out our mouths—this was not Melmac! It was—though old and chipped—china! It could break!

Everything within his reach went in: cups, saucers, silverware, platters, bowls and the last, a serving plate, which arced out over the railing, turned, caught the sun, hovered briefly over the water, a bright flash—like our summer, our childhood—turned into shadow again and dropped, unharmed, into the lake.

Margi Preus
Duluth, Minnesota

Germany was becoming very over-populated in the period from the 1840s to 1890s.

Odd Facts

Do you suppose the inspiration was Lucille Ball's movie, *The Longest Trailer?* Ohioan Joe Harrington spent three-and-a-half years building the world's largest motor home. It's twelve-and-a-half feet high, **eight feet wide** and forty-six feet long. This is a lesson in keeping an open mind about what constitutes having a good time. Take it to heart and you'll be a better person.

Indianapolis's Funny Forum once recorded an album for latch-key house-plants, including the hit, **"No Matter How Fertile,** There's No Place Like Loam." (I don't make it up; I only report it.)

Des Moines, Iowa, has hosted a Leisure Suit celebration for several years. It gives everybody a chance to pull out those coral and chartreuse synthetic garbs that they keep meaning to haul to Good Will. (And do they call it Good Will because the people there are cheerful while accepting synthetic gifts of coral and chartreuse?) **The rumor was** that the convention had served its purpose and was being fazed out, but the opportunity to dress in bad 1970s clothing for an evening is too tempting. There'll be a groundswell of support. Just watch.

Illinois stipulates that the dart games at county fairs use balloons with **a specified amount of air.** Gosh, it's only right. What unscrupulous business shark would do otherwise.

The Burlington, Wisconsin, Liars' Club has been encouraging **fibs and tall tales** since 1934. January 1 is the date of their annual gathering and broadcast. Heck of a way to start the New Year.

Robert Altman, Kansas City, Missouri: film director with accolades galore.

It was once illegal for women to **impersonate Santa Claus** in Minnesota. I guess it was one of those guy things.

W.F. "Doc" Carver, Winslow, Illinois, was a sharpshooter who joined Buffalo Bill Cody's Wild West Show. They ran it together for twenty years. In a show before **the Prince of Wales,** "Doc" shot one hundred glass balls in a row and then did almost as well from the "back of a speeding horse." I bet it made his mom nervous.

Animals running wild in the Midwest might be in trouble. Berea, Ohio, demands that they wear a taillight, if it's dark. And if **a billy goat is loose** in Wisconsin, the owner must pay the finder five dollars. Keeping a chicken in Duluth is illegal if it bothers the neighbors. And in Kansas, bare hands are not a legal tool for catching fish.

Albert Von Tilzer was born in 1878 in Indianapolis, Indiana. He composed **"Take Me Out to the Ball Game,"** but it was another twenty years before he actually attended one. Talk about delayed gratification.

The Brodhead Band from Brodhead, Wisconsin, enlisted during the Civil War and, riding in their six-horse band wagon, followed **General William T. Sherman** on his Atlanta campaign. This is probably as much fun as one can have during a war.

Forgotten by too many—the **first bowler to earn 10,000 dollars** in a tournament was Harry Smith, who accomplished his feat in 1960 at the Civic Auditorium in Omaha, Nebraska.

Johnston McCulley, born in Ottawa, Illinois, in 1883 was the creator of Zorro.

Arts and Education

What sculpture is to a block of marble,
education is to an human soul.

– Joseph Addison (1672–1719)

A culture is often judged by its knowledge and by the ways in which that knowledge is expressed. In other words, a look at education and the arts can give insights into the culture of a place. One way to view midwestern culture is to consider the many ways it's been taught, learned and nurtured, from the one-room schoolhouses to the beginning of kindergarten in America, from the Morrill Act of 1862 that funded land grant colleges to the dozens of Nobel Prize winners. Midwesterners have honored and respected education as an important tool for growth. It is as if the natural resources gave to the people of the Midwest a renewable wealth, and that wealth, in turn, allowed Midwesterners to reach for education for themselves and for their children.

Acquiring a good education has been worth a great deal to Midwesterners. Going to school, whether to elementary school, even in the earlier part of the century, or to college any time, has often demanded a great sacrifice on the part of both children and parents. The school calendar was designed to fit around the busiest time of farming, but the planting and the harvest still crossed over into studies. Doing without the extra hands of young sons to help in the fields and young daughters to help feed the threshers meant longer hours for parents. And the memories of goods reused or foregone so that a youngster could attend college help "fill" attic trunks throughout the Midwest along with photo albums and old clothes.

The importance of education was one of the fundamental beliefs of many of the immigrants who came to the Midwest. Early settlers wanted to set up schools as soon as they built their homes. When a sufficient number of families moved to an area, a school was erected. In a relatively short time, country schools freckled the land, and for generations, they served children from the first through eighth grades, after which students went to town for high school. Community schools became an important part of weekly and seasonal habits in many midwestern towns and cities. The football and basketball games, the musicals, the pot lucks, the concerts—all of them built common experiences among neighbors and friends. The schools furnished much more than an education to those who sat in the desks—they provided communities with a center of gravity.

There are 599 colleges and universities in the Midwest, several of which have many thousands of students. The schools are a mix of private and public, some emphasize humanities and some emphasize science. They are a source of pride for students, alumni, and the towns, cities, and states in which they exist.

Many of the schools foster the arts and the artists. Students are encouraged in their music, their sculpting, their painting, and their poetry. And outside of schools Midwesterners foster the arts through their support of scores and scores of independent theaters, art galleries, museums, and city or regional orchestras. Midwesterners sing opera and folk tunes and heavy metal. We go to concerts of all kinds and blues and jazz festivals. We dance—square and polka are big favorites, but you can find places to enjoy the Viennese waltz, too. And some of us write books while others compose comics or publish magazines. We go to plays and we go to movies. And a lot of Midwesterners make art—beautiful, grand, serious, fine art, or peculiar, quirky, silly art. All of this variety expresses a broad stripe of culture that reflects the Midwest. There is more variety than most Americans realize—perhaps more variety than most Midwesterners realize. But the important element that Midwesterners *do* realize is that work done in earnest deserves its due. Both traditional and modern art, whether visual, theatrical, musical, or verbal, find their audiences.

And unconventional art is honored, too. So the fellow along Highway 151 in southern Wisconsin who has taken his chainsaw and various other tools to tree trunks and carved figures for passers-by to enjoy is credited for his initiative and cleverness. Many Midwesterners are less likely to be swept away by an artist hanging a bicycle seat on the wall and calling it art. They'd find the act audacious, maybe, or a rough draft of better thinking to come.

But Midwesterners know well that not everyone thinks as they do, not everyone agrees with their beliefs. Midwesterners in general, and artists in particular, have grown accustomed, over the years, to being dismissed by "coasters," and while it might sting for a while, it's not much of a surprise.

So while education may be approaching greater and greater homogenizing nationally, a lot of the art in the Midwest is very local. Artists settle into communities the way doctors used to. They build a following of admirers, and they serve them by continuing to grow where they are rooted. We who buy their art know the artists aren't showing in

Soho or Hong Kong, but we don't care. We like their art because of what it represents and because we may know the people who produced it, and because it looks just dandy next to the "grand" reprints.

It is fitting that a painting of Grant Wood's is on the cover of this book. Besides being a Midwesterner himself and showing a midwestern father and daughter in his painting, Wood was a classic midwestern artist in that his work was dismissed as "regionalist." After living in Europe and painting in classical styles for a time, Wood returned to live and paint in Iowa. His work eventually won prizes at major art museums, and, as you may have read, our cover piece, *American Gothic,* is the second most parodied piece of art in the world (*Mona Lisa* is first), which is maybe the kind of attention the Midwest will continue to receive. For those of us who call the Midwest home, it won't matter. We know the truth about the place.

Ploughshares into Pens, Part I

Midwestern writers are plentiful. Some have gone to the East Coast to make their mark; others have written from the Midwest and endured the label of "regional writer." No matter. They've still won Pulitzers, Nobels, and fans around the world.

• • •

Mott, North Dakota is home to contemporary writer Larry Woiwode whose *Beyond the Bedroom Wall* **chronicles the life** of a midwestern family.

Carl Van Vechten was an Iowan (Cedar Rapids), who went to New York and stayed. His 1924 book, *The Tattooed Countess,* told of his boyhood in Iowa, but he gained fame in 1926 during the Harlem Renaissance for *Nigger Heaven.* It sold 100,000 copies and described life in Harlem, which, during the 1920s and up to the Depression was **a feast of music and sophisticated parties.** Van Vechten continued to enjoy success and the merry life in the East.

Edgar Lee Masters **practiced law in Chicago,** Illinois, with Clarence Darrow, before publishing the *Spoon River Anthology* in 1915. It was loosely based on people he knew in Lewiston, Illinois, and didn't make everyone happy.

James Jones (1921–1977) Robinson, Illinois, was the author of *From Here to Eternity,* which was based on his World War II experiences in the Pacific. The movie based on the book **won eight Oscars,** and because of the power of suggestion, you are probably humming the tune at this very moment.

Another Illinois writer, Edgar Rice Burroughs, was born in Chicago in 1875. His efforts into entrepreneurial adventures flopped—except writing. He decided to write **a jungle story,** and *Tarzan* was born. Burroughs was the oldest newspaper correspondent to serve in the Pacific during World War II.

Kansas has hosted 22 movies in the past decade.

Hamlin Garland, whose real first name, by the way, was Hannibal, was born to a poor family of West Salem, Wisconsin, in 1860. The family moved to the Dakota Territory and then to Iowa when he was growing up. He was **refused admission to Harvard,** so he put his midwestern ingenuity to work, attended another school in Boston, and further educated himself at the Boston Public Library. He won the 1922 Pulitzer Prize in biography for *A Daughter of Middle Border.*

One of Ohio's most famous writers is Sherwood Anderson, whose *Winesburg, Ohio* was modeled on the town where he grew up, Clyde. The book provides **intimate portraits** of Winesburg citizens and is used in classrooms as a model of literary style and skill.

One day Mark Twain found a fifty-dollar bill on the street in Keokuk, Iowa, where he was writing for the newspaper his brother owned. No one claimed the bill, so young Twain (Samuel Clemens) **decided to go to the Amazon.** He got as far as Cincinnati. It is noteworthy that the mighty Mississippi was the setting for Mark Twain's *Huckleberry Finn,* from which, some critics say, American literature sprang.

When Harriet Beecher Stowe was still Harriet Beecher and living at home in Cincinnati, Ohio, she **crossed the Ohio River** into Kentucky one day to visit a plantation and saw slavery for the first time. The event had a profound effect on her, inspiring her to write *Uncle Tom's Cabin,* and the book subsequently had a profound effect on the nation.

Ole Rolvaag (1876–1931) taught Norwegian at St. Olaf College in Northfield, Minnesota. But he is remembered primarily for his trilogy about settlement in the Dakotas. **The most famous book** in the trilogy is called *Giants in the Earth.*

One of the Midwest's most prominent writers moved from Virginia to **a farm near Red Cloud** when she was nine years old and later into town. Willa Cather captured her Nebraska experiences in *O Pioneers!* and *My Antonia.*

Ken Kercheval from Wolcottville, Indiana, played Cliff Barnes in "Dallas."

Jazz, La De Da

Jazz was developed by African-American musicians in the South in the early twentieth century. With the migration of Blacks to Chicago for work during World War I came the music. It flourished there and in Kansas City, growing and expanding in a variety of ways through musicians such as Charlie Parker and Benny Goodman.

• • •

Woody Herman was labeled "Boy Wonder of the Clarinet." Born in Milwaukee, Wisconsin, he organized his first band, **The Herd,** in 1936. He played on through the decades—blues, swing, and jazz. His greatest hit was "Woodchopper's Ball."

Chicago, Illinois' South Side has nurtured numerous jazz greats—Sidney Bechet, Benny and Harry Goodman, **Louis Armstrong,** Hoagy Carmichael, Freddie Keppard, Louis Panico, Eddie Condon, Jess Stacy, Rapolla and Teagarden, and Ben Pollack. How'd you like to stroll down the streets of your neighborhood and hear music drifting outdoors from some of those early greats?

Speaking of Benny Goodman, the jazz clarinetist, born in 1909, was one of the country's most renowned musicians. Wildly popular in the 1930s and 1940s, he was nicknamed the **"King of Swing"** and was the first jazz musician to play in the former Soviet Union. Premier Nikita Khruschev wasn't fond of his sound, but young Russians liked him. Isn't that the same old story?

The Graystone Hall of Fame and **International Jazz Museum,** as well as the Motown Historical Museum are in Detroit, Michigan. Go swing a little.

Kenosha, Wisconsinite Don Ameche was once radio announcer for Edgar Bergen.

Noble Sissle, Indianapolis, joined **Eubie Black** in 1915 to begin a long partnership of vaudeville musicianship. The two broke the "color barrier" in theater. One of their big hits was "I'm Just Wild About Harry."

Kansas City, Missouri, bought **Charlie "Bird" Parker's plastic saxophone** for 140,000 dollars for its Jazz Hall of Fame. That's hometown love.

Josephine Baker, who grew up in **East St. Louis, Illinois,** sang and performed for forty years in Paris, France, a locale friendlier to her color and her talent.

Gene Krupa, born in 1909, was another Chicago, Illinois jazz musician. His drumming brought him **national fame and prizes** and brought fans to their feet. But music was his second career; he'd first planned to become a priest, which is a different kind of drumming altogether.

Jazz great **Miles Davis,** born in 1926 in Alton, Illinois, started out as a classical trumpeter. He discovered jazz, of all the unlikely places, at the Juilliard School of Music in New York City. I wonder if it was after hours.

Quincy Jones, yet another child of Chicago, Illinois, has won more awards than any other contemporary musician. He is a trumpeter, conductor, composer, and arranger, who's been **nominated for seventy-four Grammys** and won twenty-six of them. He joined talents with Lionel Ritchie and Michael Jackson to write "We Are the World," the theme of the 1985 LiveAid concert to benefit starving children in Africa.

Indiana screenwriter Paul Osborn wrote scripts for The Yearling *and* South Pacific.

Cinematic Wonders

For some reason, it seems that everybody wants to be a movie star, at least for fifteen minutes. Here are a few examples of Midwesterners who are in the business in some fashion or other.

Movie genius Orson Welles was born in 1915 to an inventor father and a pianist mother and spent his childhood in Kenosha, Wisconsin. By age ten **he'd devoured Shakespeare's plays,** and when he was nineteen, he performed in *Romeo and Juliet* on Broadway. His film masterpiece, *Citizen Kane,* was completed in 1941 when he was twenty-six. *The Magnificent Ambersons,* a commercial failure was set in a town in the Midwest and was drawn from Welles' childhood.

A successful set of careers that began with *The Kentucky Fried Movie* (after a movie with that kind of title, where can you go but up—incidentally, the home of **Kentucky Fried Chicken** is not in Kentucky, it's in Indiana; maybe you read that already) was followed by *Airplane!* And *Naked Gun!* And *Naked Gun 2½!* (These exclamation points are not mine, by the way!) The producers are three friends who teamed up when they were students at the University of Wisconsin in Madison.

And speaking of **Madison:** *Back to School* with Rodney Dangerfield, 1986, was also filmed there.

An Indiana screenwriter named Steve Tesich won an Oscar for Breaking Away.

The Ice Pack is a group of about four hundred Minnesota natives around the country who are **now in the film industry.** They apparently keep their eyes out for opportunities to use Minnesota as a setting.

The Coen Brothers, from St. Louis Park, Minnesota, have made **quite a noise** with their movies. *Barton Fink* was one, and *Fargo* struck home in a number of ways with Midwesterners everywhere. (And it struck out with others.) Ja?

Pat O'Brien, Milwaukee, Wisconsin, starred in *Angels with Dirty Faces* and *The Boy with Green Hair,* but his **most famous role** was the lead in *Knute Rockne— All American,* which he appeared in with native Illinoisan, Ronald Reagan.

Some movies **set in the Midwest:**
INDIANA: *Hoosiers, In God We Trust, All Others Pay Cash,* and *Breaking Away*
IOWA: *Field of Dreams, Country,* and *The Bridges of Madison County*
ILLINOIS: *Ordinary People, The Fugitive, The Blues Brothers,* and *Hoop Dreams*
MINNESOTA: *Grumpy Old Men, Fargo*
SOUTH DAKOTA: *Dances with Wolves*

Sydney Pollack, Lafayette, Indiana, was a movie mogul who directed *The Way We Were, Tootsie, Out of Africa*—for which he won a **Best Director Oscar**— *Absence of Malice,* and *They Shoot Horses, Don't They?* Movies, movies, and more movies.

Howard Hawks, **Goshen, Indiana,** native, directed *Gentlemen Prefer Blondes, Bringing up Baby,* and *Scarface.*

The Joslyn Art Museum in Omaha, Nebraska, is one of the Midwest's finest.

Tales from Avon Township, North Dakota

As a young girl, my school wardrobe consisted of a homemade under-shirt with buttons, garters attached to a shirt or a set of suspenders to hold up ugly cotton stockings, and black sateen bloomers with cuffs just above the knee. Over that I wore a slip and dress, and of course we wore high-topped black shoes. The winter wardrobe was varied by long underwear—a new set once a week after the Saturday bath. As the days wore on, the wool drooped farther and farther, and it was a trick to fold them neatly at the ankle in order to pull stockings over them. Fortunately, we all dressed alike.

I guess I was about six or seven when the older boys—fourteen, fifteen, and sixteen—pulled a prank and dropped a dead mouse down my back. It fell all the way down to the cuff of my bloomers and stayed there. It was a long frightening afternoon, but I was too shy to tell the teacher. My mom took it out when I got home.

When I was in first grade, our teacher was Minnie Johnson; she'd had one year at Normal School. This was 1928–29 and women wore very short dresses. One day when she was helping a student, a boy pulled her garter and snapped it. When she tried to discipline the guilty party, the big boys jumped out the window.

My fourth, fifth, and sixth grade teacher had a Master's degree. It was the early 1930s and with the poor economy, he must have been unable to find a job beyond a rural school. He was a good teacher, and he also allowed us to skip recesses and add the time to the lunch hour. Then we could walk a half-mile to the slough and skate or slide around.

Recess games included pump-pump-pullaway and anti-over, which we played over the barn.* We also played hide-and-seek and

Nebraskan Bess Streeter Aldrich (1881–1954): A Lantern in Her Hand, The Rim of the Prairie.

competed with each other in high jumps and broad jumps. For lunch, we brought sandwiches and a potato. The potatoes sat on top of the stove baking all morning. Mothers took turns sending jars of gravy.

PTA meetings were our social events. We children recited and sang songs, and then the desks were pushed to one side and we played games—Skip to My Lou, Gustav Schol (a simple square dance), and Drop the Handkerchief. Later we had fruit nectar, coffee, cookies, and cake. The events started at eight and went until eleven or twelve. During the winter, we traveled in a bob-sled, and the family that lived farthest from school would "drive," picking up those of us who lived closer, along the way. Since the dirt roads were unusable in the winter, we put the car up on blocks and brought the battery inside, usually from November to April.

The county superintendent made unannounced visits to observe the teacher and see if things were being done right. My eighth-grade teacher had a lot of headaches, so I ended up teaching everyone but me. When the superintendent drove up, I scooted to my seat, and we all paid attention to the teacher to protect her reputation.

When public school was over for the year, we had a month of parochial school with Bible lessons, verse memorization, songs, and lessons in Norwegian. It was relaxed and fun.

I liked school. Even with a sister, I felt isolated during the summer and was eager for classes to begin again in the fall.

Adaline Lieberg
Hot Springs Village, Arkansas
(grew up near Northwood, North Dakota)

* This game is a form of catch between two groups of people. It's unusual in that it's played with one group on one side of the barn or garage and one group on the other.

From Indiana, Theodore Dreiser (1871–1945): Sister Carrie, An American Tragedy.

Don't I Know You

And here, ladies and gentlemen, are some of the most famous people in America. They began as "fly-over" people, but the world got around to noticing them eventually.

● ● ●

Johnny Carson, born in Corning, Iowa in 1925, moved on to Nebraska, where he grew up, then **on to California,** where he grew rich.

Actor Fred MacMurray was born in Kankakee, Illinois, and began his performing career as a saxophonist. In the 1930s and 1940s, **he often played the "heavy"** in movies, convincing wives to kill their husbands and other bad things. Then his comedic streak was discovered and for many years, he played the father on "My Three Sons."

Mamie Van Doren was Joan Lucille Olander in her early life; she was **born in Rowena,** South Dakota. She starred in movies in the 1950s and 1960s. Her films included *Ain't Misbehavin', High School Confidential* and *The Candidate.* Remember?

Lillian Russell was another famous person who underwent a name change. I guess it was all part of packaging at that time. She was born as Helen Louise Leonard in 1861 in Clinton, Iowa. **Known for her ravishing beauty,** she began as an opera singer and later became a pop singer and comedian.

How about that David Letterman? Something else for Indiana to boast about. Doesn't he remind you of **your older brother**—or some goofy friend of your older brother's? You gotta love him.

From Indiana, Lew Wallace: Ben-Hur: a Tale of Christ *(also governor of New Mexico Territory).*

John Wayne (1907–1979) was born in Winterset, Iowa, as Marion Michael Morrison. He made nearly two hundred films and became **an American legend.** He won the Academy Award for Best Actor in 1969 for his role in *True Grit.*

Winterset enjoyed a renewal of interest when Robert Waller's *Bridges of Madison County* hit the big time. Winterset is in Madison County, needless to say, and in addition to postcards of covered bridges, tourists can purchase a cookbook compiled by the ladies at the local church. Waller, by the way, is a guitar-strumming, post-hippie kind of guy who taught in the business school at the University of Northern Iowa in Cedar Falls, Iowa, before his fame and fortune made that unnecessary. Now, we assume, he's in bliss.

Marilyn Pauline Novak was born in 1933 in Chicago, Illinois. In Hollywood, a Columbia producer spotted her classic beauty and groomed her to replace Rita Hayworth. Marilyn became Kim, Pauline was dropped, there was **some shift in hair and eyebrows,** and in three years, the mysterious and beautiful Kim Novak was a number one box office draw.

Allen Ludden, Mineral Point, Wisconsin, was one of the first and longest-serving TV-show hosts in history. **He hosted "College Bowl"** from 1959 to 1962 and "Password" from 1962 to 1980. Way to go, Allen.

Ellen Corby, from Racine, Wisconsin, found her Hollywood success eventually, but it took a twelve-year stint as a "script girl," **vast amounts of patience,** and numerous small parts. Corby's fame came from her role as Grandma Walton, for which she was awarded several Emmys.

Emmett Kelly's famous clown character, Weary Willie, was first a character Kelly created when he was pursuing a vocation as a cartoonist. Born in Sedan, Kansas, Kelly moved to Kansas City, exhibited drawing talent, and decided that he wanted to be an artist. But then he **found work with a circus** that led to work with other circuses. You know the rest—his sad clown effectively sweeping the spotlight under the rug.

John Jakes, Chicago, Illinois: The Bastard, The Seekers, The Rebels, The Furies . . .

Rock Hudson was born Roy Scherer, Jr., in Winnetka, Illinois. He **took the name "Rock" from Gibralter.** Now that's a way to launch a career with big plans.

Ohioan Phyllis Diller was one of the **women who broke ground** for women stand-up comedians. Glory, glory, we'll never forget that hair!

The Clean-Cut Gang From Iowa

"Harriet Nelson" began life as **Peggy Lou Snyder in Des Moines, Iowa.** The question on everyone's lips is—how much did the show echo the real life of Ozzie and Harriet, or maybe the question should be how much did "The Adventures of Ozzie and Harriet" become their lives?

Sioux City, Iowa, resident Jerry Mathers, born in 1948, played **Theodore "Beaver" Cleaver** as a kid. I think there's some wise crack to be made here, but I don't know what it is.

Donna Reed from Denison, Iowa, was born in 1921. She's remembered for her own **"happy housewife" program** and for her role as Jimmy Stewart's wife in *It's A Wonderful Life.* She died in 1986, but Denison continues to celebrate Donna Reed Days.

Jessamyn West, Indiana: Friendly Persuasion.

Poetry and More

The Midwest has nurtured some very fine poets. Thank you for sharing your wisdom. We are all very proud of you.

• • •

Gwendolyn Brooks, poet and novelist, was born in Topeka, Kansas, in 1917 and raised in Chicago, Illinois. She served as **Poet Laureate of the U.S.** and was the first African-American to win the Pulitzer Prize for poetry.

Here's the quintessential, well-rounded Midwesterner: Archibald MacLeish, Glencoe, Illinois, played football, won **three Pulitzers for poetry,** served as Librarian of Congress and as Assistant Secretary of State, *and* his play, *J.B.,* about Job in modern times, was a sell-out on Broadway in 1959. How could anyone ask for any more honors and accomplishments than that!

Who was the Wisconsinite who wrote: "Laugh and the world laughs with you; Weep and you weep alone." Hint: The author **gained notoriety** for a collection of purely pulsating if not prurient poetry. Keep reading.

Vachel Lindsay, Springfield, Illinois, was **a wandering poet,** who wrote "Lincoln Walks at Midnight" and "Johnny Appleseed."

James Whitcomb Riley was **the Hoosier poet.** His hometown of Greenfield, Indiana, honors him with statuary and celebrations in the fall when "the frost is on the punkin'."

Carl Sandburg grew up in Galesburg, Illinois, graduated from neither junior high nor high school but attended Lombard College for four years. He married Laura Steichen, daughter of photographer Edward Steichen. "Fog" and *Chicago Poems* established his reputation. It was **he who baptized Chicago,** "Hog Butcher for the World."

The 1899 Cleveland National League team won only 20 games of 134. Ouch.

Paul Laurence Dunbar was born in 1872 in Dayton, Ohio. He was the only child of a couple who had successfully escaped from slavery in Kentucky and was **the only Black in his high school.** He was editor of the school newspaper and did a lot of writing as a young person. He published poetry and short stories and was recognized by important *literati* of the time, but his health was poor. He died when he was only thirty-three.

Ella Wheeler Wilcox published her first book at nine, but did not reach fame until she published *Pose(s) of Passion* in 1883. The book was criticized as immoral, but fame found her, regardless. After her husband, Robert, died, she claimed he'd "spoken" to her and directed her to go to Europe and advise World War I soldiers about their sex problems. She was off. She was a contributor for almost forty years to *Cosmopolitan* on topics such as abortion, divorce, and other **matters of interest to women.** One of her poems, "Solitude," has a famous line, which people usually ascribe to either Shakespeare or Bennett Cerf. Hmm, what could it be?

Meridel LeSeuer, Midwest legend from Minnesota and now Wisconsin, a writer who **worked for human rights** all her life. She took a different path from her cousin, Joan Crawford.

How do we honor thee? Who can count the ways. Mona Van Duyn, Rita Dove, Jorie Graham. A list of these poets' **publications and honors** would probably stretch across the state of Kansas.

And remember? "Is this heaven?" "No, it's Iowa."—Field of Dreams

The Prize

In the summer of 1934, President Franklin Delano Roosevelt was making a tailgate swing through the drought and Depression-ridden upper Midwest by train. The populace was looking to the new President for relief from the seemingly hopeless state that existed.

On the day that President Roosevelt was due to pass through Devils Lake, North Dakota, my parents found themselves in the same straits as nearly all their neighbors. They were poor and desperate, but they wanted to go to town to meet the President's train. There was enough gasoline in the car to get to town, which was about twenty-two miles away, but not enough to get home again. Although my parents were very disappointed, they resigned themselves to the fact that they would not be able to go.

Some time earlier, my mother had entered a recipe contest sponsored by *The Farmer* magazine, in which monetary prizes were to be awarded for winning entries. In the mailbox that morning was an envelope containing $3.00; *The Farmer* magazine had accepted her pie recipe!

Plans for the day changed in a hurry. Mother packed a lunch and the whole family climbed into our 1928 Studebaker and rode to Devils Lake via U.S. Highway 2. The $3.00 prize was enough to finance a trip to town for the big event.

It was a warm and pleasant day, and once in town, we waited outside the Great Northern Hotel for the train to arrive. I remember Father boosting us three children to a window sill of the Hotel so that we could see the President. It was a day that boosted our hopes and the hopes of our neighbors.

Wilton Blake Webster
Churchs Ferry, North Dakota

Miss America, 1971, was Terry Ann Meeuwsen of De Pere, Wisconsin.

188

Early Schooling

Education and its benefits have been deeply important to Midwesterners since the first settlers broke ground. The facilities haven't always been posh, but the goals and the determination to fulfill them have more than compensated for any material omissions.

• • •

Early South Dakotans **cared deeply about the education of their children.** A mere four years after the establishment of the Dakota territory, the first school district began. The year was 1865.

The school debate was a popular form of entertainment on cold winter nights before massive mass media landed in midwestern living rooms. Debates were held at the country school, and, rather than being **argued by students,** were argued by their parents. Topics were similar to those used today but with an early century twist. Resolved: The next fifty years will not see as many great inventions as the past fifty years. Or, resolved: A college education is more to be desired than a thousand dollars.

In 1925 Dr. Sidney L. Pressey, working at Ohio State University in Columbus, built the **world's first teaching machine;** it rewarded students for giving the right answer by dispensing candy. Why, many students might ask, was the

The only bullfight ever held in America was held in Dodge City, Kansas.

Palmer Handwriting Method, with its tyrannical exercises in writing o's, allowed to proliferate like crazy and the Pressey machine suppressed? We must leave such questions in the hands of historians.

The **first kindergarten in the United States** was organized in Watertown, Wisconsin, in 1856, when Margarethe Meyer Shurz brought together six children including two of her own. The concepts, of course, came from her native Germany, as did the word, "kindergarten."

How do you spell success? **Three midwestern states rank first** (Iowa), second (North Dakota), and third (South Dakota) nationally in their students' SAT (Scholastic Achievement Test) scores. It's been argued that those who take the test are a select group; most midwestern colleges require the ACT (American College Testing), so it is more widely taken. But look at this: South Dakota is at the bottom nationally for average teacher salary—$21,300, and it ranks fiftieth and forty-seventh, respectively, on school money spent per capita in the population and on the average per pupil. There is something larger going on here. I don't know what it is, but it seems the students do better than they "should." Let it be added that North Dakota teacher salaries, at 23,000 dollars, rank forty-eighth in the nation. Iowa ranks thirty-seventh with 26,700 dollars.

Especially for children—the Magic House (hands-on science) in St. Louis, Missouri.

Purdue University in West Lafayette, Indiana, hired Amelia Earhart as counselor for its women students and as a **consultant on aeronautics.** The year was 1937, two years before she disappeared.

In the early 1920s, Wendell Phillips High school in Chicago, Illinois, served young students during the day and adults in the evening. Adults could take elementary classes for one dollar and **high school classes for two dollars.** The school's night classes grew so popular that on a typical evening, there were often two thousand adults at the school.

"The Michigan System" was a plan initiated by Henry Simmons Frieze and introduced in 1871. According to the plan, **schools, instead of students, were "tested" for entrance into college.** If a student had graduated from an approved school, he or she didn't need to take an individual exam. I know some high school students who would be most pleased with this plan.

Ella Flagg Young became the first president of the National Education Association after being **the first woman to serve as superintendent of a major school system**—Chicago, Illinois'.

And now a word from one of our own . . .

What I miss most about the Midwest:

"A certain remoteness along with up-to-date communication that does not take away from one's individuality."

– LeRoy Neiman

Youngstown, Ohio, forbids citizens to ride on the outside of taxis.

Some Nobel Prize Winners Born in the Midwest

South Dakota
Ernest Orlando Lawrence ....1939 Physics
Theodore William Schultz ....1979 Economics

Nebraska
George Wells Beadle ....1958 Medicine
Val Logsdon Fitch ....1980 Physics
Lawrence Robert Klein ....1980 Economics

Kansas
James Batcheller Sumner ....1971 Medicine
Earl Wilbur Sutherland ....1971 Medicine

Missouri
Thomas Stearns Eliot..1948 Literature

Iowa
Norman Ernest Borlaug ....1970 Peace

Minnesota
Harry Sinclair Lewis ....1930 Literature
Melvin Calvin..1961 Chemistry

Wisconsin
William Parry Murphy ....1934 Medicine
Herbert Spencer Gasser...1944 Medicine
John Bardeen(2) ....1956 Physics
                                                                                1972 Physics
Herbert Alexander Simon..1978 Economics

Illinois
Robert Andrews Millikan ....1923 Physics
Laura Jane Addams ....1931 Peace
Clinton Joseph Davisson..1937 Physics
Gerard Debreu ....1943 Medicine

In 1906, the Chicago White Sox were fondly known as "The Hitless Wonders."

Edward Adelbert Doisy ....1943 Medicine
Edward Mills Purcell ....1952 Physics
Ernest Miller Hemingway ....1954 Literature
Vincent Du Vigneaud ....1955 Chemistry
James Dewey Watson ....1962 Medicine
Robert William Holley ....1968 Medicine
Stanford Moore ....1972 Chemistry
John Robert Schrieffer...1972 Physics
Paul John Flory ....1974 Chemistry
Benjamin Roy Mottelson ....1975 Physics
James Watson Cronin ....1980 Physics
James Tobin ....1981 Economics
Jerome I. Friedman ....1990 Physics
Harry M. Markowitz ....1990 Physics

Michigan
Ralph Johnson Bunche ....1950 Peace
Glenn Theodore Seaborg ....1951 Chemistry
Thomas Huckle Weller ....1954 Medicine
Alfred Day Hershey ....1969 Medicine
Samuel Chao Cung Ting ....1976 Physics

Indiana
Harold Clayton Urey ....1934 Chemistry
Wendell Meredith Stanley ....1946 Chemistry
Paul Anthony Samuelson ....1970 Economics
Philip Warren Anderson ....1977 Physics

Ohio
Charles Gates Dawes ....1925 Peace
Arthur Holly Compton ....1927 Physics
Donald Arthur Glaser ....1960 Physics
William Nunn Lipscomb ....1976 Chemistry
Toni Morrison ....1993 Literature

Don't gloat, but a proud, happy glow seems in order.

In 1906, the Chicago White Sox won the World Series. A near miracle.

Sometimes You Get What You Want

ANNA WRIGHT, mother of Frank Lloyd Wright, wanted an architect for a child. When she was pregnant, she read about architecture and studied drawings. And she decorated baby Frank's nursery with ten drawings of cathedrals. It worked; her infant grew up to be the most prominent U.S. architect of the twentieth century.

Wright became a draftsman for Louis Sullivan in Chicago, but he was displeased about the design of the Chicago World's Fair transportation building and left the firm in 1893, when he was in his early twenties. At that point he began developing the style that he's associated with today. He believed that buildings should harmonize with their surroundings and, whenever possible, he used materials available in the local area. He also did amazing things with concrete. (See books in your local library for the visuals here.)

Wright spent much of his life in southwestern Wisconsin on an estate he named Taliesin. His first home burned, he rebuilt it and then that one burned as well. He rebuilt again but this third one he lost to bankruptcy; friends and clients helped him out, and in 1929, it was returned to him.

Twenty-five of the 120 buildings in the Frank Lloyd Wright Historic district in Oak Park, Illinois, were designed by Wright himself. The Willits house, completed in 1920 in Highland Park, introduced the long, low style that became the classic "prairie style."

Before his death in 1959, Wright designed a mile-high skyscraper. No one's tried to build it yet. (The Sears Tower is 1,454 feet, so that's 3,826 *additional* feet. Way up there.)

Omaha, Nebraska, hosts snowball softball and 75 national teams compete.

Ploughshares into Pens, Part II

Lorraine Hansberry, who grew up in Chicago, Illinois, was **the first African-American woman to have a play on Broadway.** *A Raisin in the Sun* was produced when Hansberry was twenty-nine.

Zona Gale, born in Portage, Wisconsin, in 1874, was one of the first female reporters in Milwaukee, Wisconsin. She wrote *Miss Lulu Bett,* the story of an unmarried woman. The book was a best seller the same year that Sinclair Lewis's *Main Street* was published. *Miss Lulu Bett* was adapted as a play and won a Pulitzer Prize in 1921. Lewis, by the way, who grew up in Sauk Centre, Minnesota, was **the first American to win the Nobel Prize for literature.** That happened in 1930.

Raymond Chandler, legendary writer from Chicago, Illinois, invented the much-loved and **often-imitated Philip Marlowe** in *The Big Sleep.* For readers on the edge of their chairs, it was The Big Awake.

Iowan Susan Allen Toth, now of St. Paul, Minnesota, wrote about growing up **in the middle of the country.** The book was titled, appropriately enough, *Blooming.*

Edna Ferber's triumph was a book-turned-musical (that's been revived again) called *Showboat.* Ferber lived in Ottumwa, Iowa, for seven years of her childhood, and in later years said **exposure to the Des Moines and Mississippi rivers influenced the book.** She graduated from high school in Appleton,

The first national archery association was begun in Crawfordsville, Indiana in 1879.

Wisconsin, and was a reporter before turning to novels and plays. She won a Pulitzer in 1924 for *So Big*.

F. Scott Fitzgerald, one of America's foremost writers in the early twentieth century *(The Great Gatsby, Tender Is the Night)* was born and raised in St. Paul, Minnesota. **His rival or colleague,** depending on their moods, Ernest Hemingway, was born in Oak Park, Illinois. Hemingway, born in 1899, signed up as a Red Cross ambulance driver during World War I because he had a bad eye and was turned down for regular service. Although he wanted it desperately, he didn't win the Pulitzer until 1953 after *The Old Man and the Sea* was published. The following year he won the Nobel Prize for literature.

The University of Iowa's Writers Workshop in Iowa City, Iowa, claims as former students such writers as **Flannery O'Connor,** Gail Godwin, John Irving, and Kurt Vonnegut.

Humorist Bill Nye may not be as famous as Mark Twain, but he used to tour with him and with Artemus Ward (a humorist who used puns and misspellings to accentuate his **deadpan style,** which influenced Twain) and James Whitcomb Riley. Nye wrote columns where he practiced his frontier humor and is considered one of the founders of such humor. He came to Wisconsin as a small child and grew up on a farm near Grantsburg.

Thorton Wilder, born in Madison, Wisconsin, in 1897, chose to write about simple things, not, as he apparently once said, **"the adulteries of dentists."** The results were *The Bridge of San Luis Rey, Our Town,* and *The Skin of Our Teeth,* which brought him Pulitzers and other prizes, including the Presidential Medal of Freedom in 1963. So we must still await tales of dastardly dentists.

From 1896 to 1921, Iowa banned the sale of cigarettes.

Happy Tune Time

Music on the prairie. Many Midwesterners have given us the gift of their music. What a joy it is. Sing out and play on.

• • •

Wisconsinite Pee Wee King made it big as both a musician/composer—with "Tennessee Waltz"—and as a **cowboy star** with Gene Autry, Charles Starrett, and others from the 1930s through the 1950s. He also hosted a variety show in 1955.

Illinoisan Cole Porter studied to be a lawyer; his grandfather bribed him with the promise of a fortune to encourage him, but he was distracted from his law school coursework by **the musical muse.** Porter loved composing, and it's a happy thing for the rest of us. "Night and Day," "Don't Fence Me In," and musicals such as "Kiss Me Kate" and "Can-Can" were a few of his successes. At age forty-five, Porter fell from a horse and his legs were badly damaged. He endured thirty-three operations and lived a painful existence until his death in 1964.

The five Jackson brothers, Jermaine, Jackie, Marlon, Tito, and Michael, from Gary, Indiana, first sang under the name **Ripples and Waves.** Their debut smash hit in 1969 with Motown Records was "I Want You Back."

Kalamazoo, Michigan, has, at one time or another made it **against the law** to serenade one's love from outside his or her window. Beware.

Prairie Island, Minnesota, is one of several places where tribes have built casinos.

Meredith Willson, eighty-two years at his death in 1984, was born in Mason City, Iowa. The town was immortalized as **River City** in his Broadway musical, "The Music Man." But you knew that.

Missourian Margaret Tobin Brown, who **survived the sinking Titanic,** was immortalized in the musical, "The Unsinkable Molly Brown."

The 1945 hit "Peg O' My Heart" was by the Chicago group, **Harmonicats.**

Paul McCartney bought the rights to the song "On Wisconsin!" and then sold it to Michael Jackson (a Midwesterner, at least). Can you believe it? I think it bears repeating. Paul McCartney bought the rights to "On Wisconsin!" and then sold it to Michael Jackson. Who sold it in the first place and why is what I don't know. **You grammarians are wondering** whether it's "On Wisconsin!" or "On, Wisconsin!" Me, too. I ran a librarian ragged seeking the answer, and there were two answers. That's how life is sometimes.

Sam Cooke, **born in Chicago,** Illinois, in 1935, hit the national scene at age twenty-two with "You Send Me."

"If You Leave Me Now" launched Chicago (the musical group) to fame in 1976. Chicago (the group), of course, from Chicago (the city), was originally the Chicago Transit Authority, but **Mayor Richard Daley** was upset because there already was a CTA, and its business was transportation, not music. You may recall that when Richard Daley ordered something done, it generally was done and fast. He said to change the name. The boys cooperated.

"Come Home, Father" was a 1864 hit by Chicago, Illinois, songwriter and publisher **Henry Clay Work** that became popular with temperance workers in the next century.

A stone monument at Clear Lake, Iowa, honors **Buddy Holly,** Richie Valens,

Ride in an Amish buggy in Middlebury, Indiana.

and the Big Bopper, who died in a plane crash after playing at the Clear Lake Ballroom in 1959. And Lake Mendota in Madison, Wisconsin, was the site of the plane crash that killed Otis Redding.

Duke, Duke, Duke is not a call to fight or a repetitive lesson in **British levels of royal titles.** Remember? It's the opening of Chicago, Illinoisan Eugene Dixon's—a.k.a. Gene Chandler—hit, "Duke of Earl." Oh, the good old days.

Cleveland, Ohio, site of the splendid **Rock 'n Roll Hall of Fame and Museum**—all 150,000 square feet.

Some Milwaukee, Wisconsin, musicians from recent decades include **Steve Miller,** Boz Scaggs, the Bo Deans and the Violent Femmes. (Maybe we need to have a talk about group names and audience appeal and how the old days are different from the new days.)

Q: Who never played rock and roll but was inducted into the Rock 'n Roll Hall of Fame?

A: Les Paul, for inventing the electric guitar. Born in Waukesha, Wisconsin, as Lester Polfus, he and his wife, Mary Ford, also a Waukesha native and also known first by another name—Irene Colleen Summers—had a long musical career. They enjoyed two major hits: "How High the Moon" in 1951 and "Vaya con Dios" in 1953.

Try Halsted or Clark streets in Chicago, Illinois, for great blues music.

Kiddie Lit—Yahoo!

It happens that a lot of classic children's literature was written by Midwesterners. I would not venture to guess why that is the case, but I join those who say that some of the best literature is literature intended for children (Eugene Field's mistake notwithstanding—read on).

• • •

Laura Ingalls Wilder, **daughter of the Midwest,** was born near Pepin, Wisconsin. Her father, in the true Midwest tradition, moved the family to Kansas, Minnesota, South Dakota, and Iowa. It's no wonder that she didn't begin writing in earnest until after all the moving stopped. She was sixty-five when she published her first book, *Little House in the Big Woods.* Her daughter, Rose Wilder Lane, was born in DeSmet, South Dakota, in 1887. Rose wrote stories for the *Saturday Evening Post* and novels, including *Let the Hurricane Roar* and *Old Home Town.* Laura wrote nine of her books at her farm in Mansfield, Missouri, where she lived for over sixty years. She was shocked by the huge success of her books, saying she'd just been writing about how to be ". . . happy with simple pleasures and to be cheerful and have courage when things go wrong." Admirable goals.

When L. Frank Baum of *Wizard of Oz* fame lived in Aberdeen, South Dakota, he edited the *Saturday Pioneer Newspaper* there. Some believe his South Dakota experiences were used in the book. Hmmm, let's see. Wind, dust, tornadoes, fairs, and balloons. Not to mention farm hands, little dogs, and **grumpy women on bicycles.** Perhaps some material did come from Aberdeen, though most residents are optimistic and cheerful. Go visit.

Eugene Field was a newspaper columnist, who wrote *A Little Book of Western Verse* in 1889. He intended the book as a satire of Chicago big-wigs, but poems like "Little Boy Blue" and **"Winken, Blynken and Nod"** became popular chil-

Scottsbluff, Nebraska, once prohibited the storing of snowballs in refrigerators.

dren's poems, and to his dismay, he never escaped the reputation as a writer of children's poetry. Serves him right.

Clarence E. Mulford, born in Streator, Illinois, introduced Hopalong Cassidy in 1907 in the novel, *Bar-20*. What followed were **many novels and then radio** shows, movies, and television programs. Was he not one of the great innocent cowboy heroes?

Shel Silverstein, Chicago, Illinois, gave all of us "The Giving Tree" and he promulgates **mischief and laughter** over and over with *Where the Sidewalk Ends* and *A Light in the Attic*. Only brave parents dare read the advice about tossing eggs onto the ceiling.

Marguerite Henry, born in Milwaukee, Wisconsin, won first place and twelve dollars for a story when she was eleven years old. This made her think that writing would be an easy and pleasurable way to make a living. And it eventually worked. As a young woman, she had a job as a proofreader at **her father's publishing company,** which was probably useful to her. Her books, including *Misty of Chincoteague* and numerous others, have sold in the millions all over the world. She won a Newbery in 1949 for *King of the Wind*.

Sterling North, who grew up in Wisconsin, was author of *So Dear To My Heart*, a 1947 best seller about the Midwest. He also wrote *Rascal*, which drew from his childhood in Wisconsin, and which Walt Disney made into a movie called *Heart*. North had **wanted to be a prizefighter** but he contracted polio, which eliminated the possibility of a life in sports.

Ross Lockridge, Jr., Indiana: Raintree County.

Motown

MOTOWN has become the catchword for an entire movement of music made popular by African-Americans in the 1960s and 1970s. Its strong beat and use of orchestral accompaniment created a blues sound that was distinctive and rich.

By no coincidence the music was rooted in Motown Records, begun by Berry Gordy, Jr. in 1959. Gordy worked in the car industry in Detroit, Michigan, and composed songs in his free time, including "Lonely Teardrops" in 1956. Inspired by the growing popularity of rhythm and blues, he decided to move beyond just writing songs and started a recording company. Motown Records became a family business; several of the Gordys were employed there. The company became a family business in another way in that many of the artists who recorded for the label said joining Motown was like joining a family. Gordy took care of his artists, but he also had high expectations of them.

Smokey Robinson, at nineteen, was the company's first star and the only artist who later became a company executive. Other stars included Marvin Gaye, Diana Ross, Stevie Wonder, and the Jackson Five. Eventually Gordy went to California and produced movies, including *Lady Sings the Blues* and *Mahogany.*

Esther Gordy Edwards, Berry's sister, was a keeper of things, and she decided that its history deserved to be preserved and shared. In 1988, Esther opened the Motown Historical Museum in the house in Detroit where everything had begun nearly thirty years earlier.

The museum, which displays everything from Michael Jackson's diamond-studded glove to the first Motown recording studio, has thousands of visitors every year.

Traverse City, Michigan, offers more than 17 championship golf courses!

College Firsts

Greencastle, Indiana, was the site of the **first college sorority,** which began January 27, 1870.

The **first college commencement exercises within a prison** occurred in 1975 in Jackson, Michigan, when twenty degrees were granted.

Antioch College, a nonsectarian school begun in Yellow Springs, Ohio, in 1852, and presided over by Horace Mann, was the first school not affiliated with a religion where equal rights were granted to female students. And **more good news from Antioch,** where the first female college professor was granted the same privileges as men, including being able to go to faculty meetings, which was usually a male-only business. The pioneer was Rebecca Mann Pennell. She was professor of physical geography, drawing, natural history, civil history, and didactics. What an accomplished woman. I'd say that Antioch got off on the right foot.

The University of Chicago in Chicago, Illinois, has had as faculty members, Enrico Fermi, Thorstein Veblen, Milton Friedman, and John Dewey. The school **initiated correspondence courses** in 1892.

Fargo-Moorhead (North Dakota/Minnesota) has 10 golf courses.

Michigan State University in East Lansing was the nation's **first land grant university.** From its original three buildings, it has grown to a 5,320-acre complex.

The first biography course was in a biography department at Carleton College in Northfield, Minnesota. It was organized by **Ambrose White Vernon** in the school year of 1919–20.

Oberlin College, founded in 1833, deserves note for being **the first coed institution** in the nation and for inviting people of all races to enroll. Also noteworthy is the fact that it began the first department of music in the country in 1865.

America's **first dental school** was founded in Bainbridge, Ohio, in 1928 by Dr. John Harris. We might all give a word of thanks for that development.

The **first Black woman college graduate** was Lucy Ann Stanton from Cleveland, Ohio. She graduated from Oberlin in 1850.

The **University of Michigan at Ann Arbor** was the first state university supported by a direct property tax.

The first state university to **grant equal privileges to women** was Indiana University in Bloomington. Sarah Parke Morrison was the first woman to enter the school—in 1869—and the first to graduate.

Lincoln, Nebraska, has three days (!) of polka fun in August. You can go.

Journalism

Midwestern journalists and journalism in the Midwest have both been important and successful. The cause may be linked to the valued position held by education. Journalism, after all, is a public form of teaching and learning. The people and publications deserving note are almost innumerable; here's a little sampling.

● ● ●

Roger Ebert, the only movie critic to win a Pulitzer Prize for his work, was born and raised in Urbana, Illinois. He is probably the **best-paid movie critic** ever, but it would be rude to ask, so that's just speculation.

Former anchor of ABC's "World News Tonight," Frank Reynolds, was **born in East Chicago, Illinois.** He won both a Peabody and an Emmy for his reporting.

Jane Pauley, from Indianapolis, Indiana, moved from Chicago's WMAQ to "Today" to her own show "Real Life with Jane Pauley" and on to "Dateline" with Stone Phillips, **a native of St. Louis,** Missouri.

Some Midwest columnists: The late Erma Bombeck, Dave Barry (born in Chicago), Mike Royko, and, of course, **the kind and wonderful Bob Greene.** Yeah!

William Allen White (1869–1944) grew up in Emporia, Kansas. He became an outspoken and articulate columnist for the Emporia Gazette and his liberal Republican views were quoted across the country. His "grass-roots" political opinions epitomized much of Midwest thinking, and his autobiography, published two years after his death, is considered a **highly valuable document** on the growth of the Midwest.

Tom Brokaw, well-known NBC news anchor, was born in Webster, South Dakota.

Mark Delahay, whose wife was a cousin of Abe Lincoln's and who had been a newspaperman and lawyer, is apparently the man who raised the volunteer force that **drove the Mormons out of St. Joseph, Missouri,** and set them on their trek to Salt Lake City, Utah. He went to Kansas to support the Free-State movement and began a newspaper. Proslavery people attacked his office and threw his press into the Missouri River.

Legendary Chicago, Illinois, journalist **Studs Terkel,** has educated us on workers and on the elderly.

The country's first abolitionist newspaper, **"The Philanthropist,"** began printing in 1817 in Mount Pleasant, Ohio.

Girard, Kansas, was home to Emanuel Haldeman-Julius, who first published a Socialist newspaper in 1919, and then printed two pamphlets with works by Oscar Wilde and *The Rubaiyat* of Omar Khayyam. The popularity of the dime publications lead him to publish classics and philosophy in what became The Little Blue Books. By 1931, 1,666 titles were or had been in print. At their peak in 1949, they sold half a million nationally, and by 1974 more than three hundred million had been sold. **Three hundred million good reads for a dime!** My question is: Where are they all?

The very first fax machine was developed at the University of Missouri in 1948 as **a means to transfer information** into the newsroom at the journalism school.

In 1866 the Cincinnati, Ohio Reds became the world's first professional baseball team.

The State Fair

August—the hottest, stickiest time of year in southern Illinois. But I had more reason to sweat than just the weather. I was in the back seat of our family sedan, with my mother and Marge, my music teacher, in the front. We were on our way from my hometown to Springfield, Illinois, to compete in the state organ competition. I had been practicing for weeks on someone else's organ, which was larger than the little organ we had at home or in the back of the music shop where Marge gave lessons. The fact that I had practiced at all was a real change from my regular visits to the music shop, where, as I entered, my heart sank in time with the tinkling of the bell over the door.

Marge was a statuesque woman with a perfect red beehive and the patience of a saint. How she, a talented organist, could tolerate week after week of my tortured and obviously unpracticed performances is more than I could understand. But no amount of guilt could make me practice—I just couldn't do it. And the only way I could get through those humiliating lessons was with the promise of a cherry Coke and a ham salad sandwich which awaited me at the drugstore's lunch counter next to the music shop.

But I was ready today—ready to take on those players from Chicago whom Marge said always won the competition. No one could play "Puff the Magic Dragon" with such style and panache as me.

We pulled into the parking lot and made our way to the cavernous auditorium. My stomach was in a knot. As the competitors climbed to the stage and performed their pieces, my breathing became shallower and shallower. I was filled with such dread that I don't even remember my turn, except for one brief moment of looking down at my hands on the keys.

In 1920, the National Football League was organized in Columbus, Ohio.

When it was over, I was sure I'd done horribly and disappointed Marge. But I was so relieved to be finished that I headed back to my seat as quickly as I could without actually running. Eager to see Mother's and Marge's reaction, my eyes were on them and I tripped and rapped my head on the seats in front of them. Through the stars and the ringing in my ears, I heard Marge say that I did just fine, but that the judge would probably give those medals to players from Chicago like he always did.

Secure in the presence of a ready excuse for failure, I was able to lean back and allow my mother to rub my head. My day was made when I won third place in the competition.

With my ribbon clutched in my hand, a lump on my head, and the memory of Marge's proud smile, I rode blissfully home.

Tamara Traeder
Berkeley, California
(born and raised in Quincy, Illinois)

And now a word from one of our own . . .

What I value about having grown up in the Midwest is:

The normative moral standard, understandable and applicable to everybody, never changed, because it was based on a standard, the Bible, and though I found that restrictive at times, it was a basis for understanding my neighbors (and treating them as I would like to be treated), and that basis of standard keeps me from some of the excesses that have taken away so many (already) of my freewheeling generation.

– LARRY WOIWODE, author

Bed races seem to be a midwestern phenomenon. Something to look into.

Some Great Minds

Buster Keaton was **born backstage** in Piqua, Kansas, when his parents were touring with Harry Houdini. Buster, who never used a double for his pratfalls, reportedly received his name from Houdini, who remarked when the six-month-old lad fell downstairs, "What a buster!"

Brothers Carl and Mark Van Doren were born in Hope, Illinois, in 1885 and 1894. **Both of them won Pulitzers**—Carl, for his biography of Benjamin Franklin in 1938, and Mark for his *Collected Poems* in 1939. Mark was the father of Charles, whose sad fate lay in the quiz show scandal.

Sam Shepard (Rogers) was born in Fort Sheridan, Illinois. His play, *Rock Garden,* became *Oh! Calcutta,* **the first large-scale musical that included nudity**. In 1979, he won a Pulitzer for *Buried Child.* He has appeared in movies, such as *Country* and *Places in the Heart,* with his wife, Jessica Lange (also a Midwesterner).

Father Flanagan was one of the Midwest's angels. He opened Overlook Farm in Omaha, Nebraska, in 1917 for **homeless and troubled boys.** Since 1979, Boys Town has become home for needy girls, too.

The first blood transfusion happened **less than a century ago.** Dr. George Crile performed the feat in Cleveland, Ohio, in 1905. (I realize that readers picking up this worn paperback in 2006 will be shaking their heads and arguing the point. Lighten up. This is how it is *now.*)

Sports personality Pat O'Brien was born in Sioux Falls, South Dakota, in 1948.

Wiseacres

We were going to call this section "Smart Alecks," but that phrase is the kind I used to get in trouble for repeating when I was a child. I could get away with "wiseacre." And, anyway, maybe its reference to land is rooted in some midwestern sentence somewhere. Whatever you call them, you know these people and they can be mighty funny.

● ● ●

Cloris Leachman, Des Moines, Iowa, won an Academy Award for Best Supporting Actress for her role in *The Last Picture Show*. And then, for **something completely different,** she played the character of Phyllis Lindstrom (remember that cheery whine?) on "The Mary Tyler Show" and in her own offshoot show. And how could we forget Frau Brukner in *Young Frankenstein?*

Richard Pryor, Peoria, Illinois, was born in 1940 and was raised primarily by his grandmother, who also ran a brothel. Perhaps the wit of the surroundings contributed to his **snappy, street-corner humor,** the kind that often elicited media blips. His comedy albums won Grammys. Talk about living up to the idea of *not* playing in Peoria.

Jerry Silberman, Milwaukee, Wisconsin, won an Oscar nomination for *The Producers*. He also acted in **Blazing Saddles,** *Willie Wonka and the Chocolate Factory, Silver Streak,* and *Haunted Honeymoon*. Who was he:
        a. Rocky Marciano **b.** John D. Rockefeller **c.** Gene Wilder

Chicago, Illinois' Second City comedy group is the progeny of an earlier theater group, Compass Players, and was started in a storefront near the University of Chicago in 1959 by Paul Sills and Bernie Sahlins. **John Belushi,** Paul Sand, Bill Murray, and Shelley Long are just a few of the talents who sharpened their wit and delivery performing with the group.

Ohio has 172 state parks, and only 2 of them have neither river nor lake.

Next time you hear the phrase, "the luck of the Irish," think of this drop-out extraordinaire from Milwaukee, Wisconsin, and shake your head in wonder. **Spencer Tracy** skipped school so much that he attended fifteen different schools in the city before he made it through elementary school. Incredible! He dropped out of high school, he dropped out of college (Ripon College), he dropped out of acting school. In between he joined the Navy with friend and future actor Pat O'Brien. He drank a lot in the 1930s in Hollywood and was not cast into parts that led anywhere, but a switch to MGM changed his career. He married Louise Treadwell and left her, but as a devout Catholic never divorced her.

And now a word from one of our own . . .

What I value most about the Midwest is:

The people are unassuming, down-to-earth, friendly, no-nonsense, helpful, kind and generally just nice people.

– Phyllis Diller

More than 6,000,000 tourists visit South Dakota annually. So there.

Moments of Greatness
(COLLEGE TALES)

The steps of **Knox College** in Galesburg, Illinois, became the site of the fifth and most famous debate between Lincoln and Douglas. The event drew 20,000 people; trainfuls came from Chicago and Iowa.

Ann Arbor, Michigan, acquired the University of Michigan from Detroit in 1837. The school wields a large influence in the city, especially through athletics. The University has one of the largest college stadiums in the country and seats over 100,000 people. Also on campus the **Baird Carillon bells** range from twenty-one pounds to twelve tons. Weekly concerts can be heard all over town—and probably beyond.

It makes sense, doesn't it, that Florida, ranking first in the percentage of population over sixty-five, ranks last as to the number of institutions of higher learning per 100,000 people. So **it's surprising** that North Dakota, which ranks eighth for its percentage of population over sixty-five, ranks first in number of institutions of higher education per 100,000. (So at the next cocktail party when you're told that New York has 214 such institutions, you might note that North Dakota's fourteen colleges and universities represent a higher percentage.)

In 1892, the University of Chicago opened its doors in Hyde Park, Illinois, with 103 faculty and 594 students. (Many schools were opening with fifty students and four or five faculty, so this opening was grand indeed.) The school was endowed by the **American Baptist Education Association** and by money from the Rockefellers. In addition, the school was given land by Marshall Field. All of that makes for a handsome way to begin a school.

Indiana University's Lilly Library has one of the finest collections of rare books (over 100,000) in the country. They include the New Testament section of a

Olivia, Minnesota, celebrates corn. They have a Bunyanesque cob monument.

Gutenberg Bible and documents relating to the discovery of the New World and early American history.

Josiah Bushness Grinnell (1821–1891) was a clergyman, pioneer, politician, and abolitionist. He moved from New England to Iowa in 1854. It was Grinnell to whom Horace Mann gave that oft-repeated phrase **"Go west, young man"** when Grinnell sought advice about how to best fulfill the mission of his life. Grinnell founded the acclaimed college—Grinnell—that is located in Grinnell, Iowa. He served as a U.S. Representative from 1863 to 1867.

Gumption, foresight, and faith in action: North Western University (now Northwestern University) in **Chicago, Illinois,** opened in 1851 with ten pupils. Illinois State Normal (now Illinois State University) opened in 1857 with nineteen pupils.

In 1867 Urbana, Illinois "won" the Illinois Industrial College. The town gained the right to have what is now the University of Illinois by offering land, a building, landscaping, and **substantial free freight on the railway.** It opened in 1868 with three teachers and fifty students. Students were expected to contribute two hours daily to build fences, to keep out livestock, and to construct sidewalks, furniture, and roads. How times have changed.

Private midwestern universities **among the top in the nation** include the University of Chicago, Northwestern, George Washington, Notre Dame, Loyola, McCallister, DePaul, Grinnell, Antioch, Oberlin, and more.

For some folks, picking their own fruit is a special kind of fun. Yup.

First, An Idea

Long before a picture or a sculpture or any work of art takes shape, some jolt occurs in an artist's mind. What do you suppose that's all about? Fortunately, we can appreciate the results without having to understand the entire process. Here are a few reminders of midwestern artistry.

● ● ●

Gutzon Borglum (1867–1941) was a sculptor whose works are remembered better than his name. It was he who **carved the likenesses** of Presidents Washington, Jefferson, Roosevelt (Teddy), and Lincoln on Mount Rushmore. (Jefferson was supposed to be on the other side of Washington, but a misdirected blast removed the critical part of the rock, so Borglum had to change the arrangement to the present order.)

Thomas Hart Benton, born in Neosho, Missouri, was the son of a Congressman, and the grand-nephew and namesake of Senator Benton, who served Missouri for thirty years. Young Thomas studied art in Chicago and Paris, taught at Ivy League schools, and then traveled the South and Midwest before settling in Kansas. His work, which **depicts life in the Midwest** was dubbed Regionalism, a label he shared with Grant Wood and John Steuart Curry. Its style was described as having linear design and cartoonish, flat characters. "Threshing Wheat" is one of his best-known works. He died in 1975 at the age of eighty-six.

LeRoy Neiman, Chicago, Illinois, is to **sports-based art** (Olympics posters, postage stamps, and more) what Georgia O'Keeffe was to flowers.

Frederick Remington came to Kansas at the age of twenty-two because a friend of his had convinced him that **raising sheep could be fun.** Remington had inherited more than 10,000 dollars when his father died, and he wanted to "get

You can see dinosaur bones in 5 places in North Dakota, even a steakhouse.

rich." Sheep ranching, however, didn't work out so well, and neither did his investment in a Kansas City saloon. (What he needed were more reliable advisors.) Meanwhile, he sketched and sketched and sketched. Artworks began selling, and eventually led to his earning a reputation equal to Charles Russell for documenting life in the Old West. There's a lesson here about putting all of one's eggs in one basket. The advice seems to be: Don't.

Owen Gromme, Wisconsin's **famous wildlife artist,** won the competition for the Federal Duck Stamp Design in 1945.

Claes Oldenburg, who spent many years of his childhood in Chicago, Illinois, is a sculptor of unusual objects. He **created a huge umbrella**—or the outline of an umbrella—for downtown Des Moines, Iowa, and there's a giant hollow baseball bat in downtown Chicago.

John Stueart Curry was born on a farm near Dunavent, Kansas, and became that state's greatest painter. You've seen his paintings of **storms and cyclones,** I'm sure.

Georgia O'Keeffe, born in Sun Prairie, Wisconsin, in 1896, attended the Sacred Heart Academy in Madison. Her painting style was termed unconventional, but she wanted to paint what was in her head, not what was presented to her. A friend took some of her work to Alfred Stieglitz in New York, who included her work in one of his **unconventional shows in 1916,** and the rest, as they say, is history. She painted New York City scenes, but her most famous work is of desert images—stylized animal skulls and flowers that are oversized and yet intimate. O'Keeffe died in New Mexico in 1986.

Persons aged 25 or over in the Midwest with bachelor's degree or greater: 32,310,253.

Helen Farnsworth Mears, whose mother was Wisconsin's first poet, was a sculptor who received her **first big commission** when she was twenty and carved a nine-foot marble statue called Genius of Wisconsin for the Wisconsin Building at Chicago's 1893 World Exposition.

Harry Hamilton Bennett began a photography business that is the oldest family-operated photo business in the United States. Bennett, who lived in Kilbourn, Wisconsin, and later, in the Wisconsin Dells, is considered one of the three **best landscape photographers** of the nineteenth century. In 1890 or so, he was one of the first to use stop-action photography.

In the mid-1800s, a twenty-year-old named Vinnie Ream from Madison, Wisconsin, moved to Washington, D.C., to apprentice with sculptor Clark Mills. Her talents were recognized and rewarded. She sculpted busts of General Custer and John Sherman, and in 1864 Congressional friends arranged for her to sculpt Lincoln. He first refused, but when he learned the request came from a young lady trying to earn a living, he consented and **posed for thirty minutes** a day for five months. In 1866, she received a 10,000-dollar commission to sculpt Lincoln for the Capitol Rotunda. It was unveiled in 1871 and described as "Lincoln all over."

MacKinlay Kantor, Webster City, Iowa: Andersonville, *Pulitzer Prize in 1956.*

Those Radio Guys

Some of the first radio stations in the country were built in the Midwest. The device was a boon to farmers, not only for the weather reports that began drifting in but for the added communication. Radio voices became "best friends" for many an isolated farm family.

• • •

Bruce Beemer from Mount Carmel, Illinois was **the first Lone Ranger** on the radio. Another Illinoisan, Clayton Moore, from Chicago, took over in 1949.

Garrison Keillor keeps us amused from St. Paul, Minnesota, most of the time; and then there's that absent-minded guy who does the radio show, **Whaddya Know?** from Madison, Wisconsin—Michael Feldman.

Jack Benny, was **Benny Kubelsky** from Waukegan, Illinois. He began in vaudeville and moved on to radio, then to Hollywood and TV. Do you suppose he did that arm-folding trick in vaudeville performances and then returned to it when he was on camera again?

Don McNeill of "Breakfast Club" fame turned an early morning chat time into a wholesome variety show with tunes to drink your coffee with and songs to inspire the kids to **march around the breakfast table.** McNeill was born in Galena, Illinois, and raised in Wisconsin.

Edgar Berggren was born in Chicago, Illinois. He dropped a few letters from his last name, adopted **a wooden dummy** carved by a man named Charlie Mack, and the winning pair became known as Edgar Bergen (father of Candace) and Charlie McCarthy—1950s radio and TV favorites.

John G. Neihardt, Nebraska: Black Elk Speaks, *1932.*

Odd Facts

In 1887, women were allowed to vote in city races in Kansas. There was a tremendous turnout, and Susana Salter was **elected as the mayor of Argonia.** I'll bet her relatives are proud.

Controversial artifact: The Kensington Runestone is a rectangular-shaped stone that bears inscriptions indicating that Norsemen penetrated deep into North America nearly a century before Columbus, if you believe them. Critics question its discovery, its inscription, and the timing of its appearance— following a declaration by a Norwegian historian that the Norse hadn't come to North America, *and* after a replica ship made the trip from Bergen, Norway, to the New World. Nevertheless, **the stone is accorded respect;** the original is displayed at the Smithsonian, and it's replicated for Minnesota museums, the state where it was unearthed.

The Indiana General Assembly once debated changing the value of *pi* from 3.1416 to three, since **it was easier to work with.** A sound principle, but some mediocre thinking.

Iowa City, Iowa, has long enjoyed the boast of having **more college degrees per capita than any other city in the country.** You're likely to overhear drug-store clerks discussing Rilke's poetry or the ideas of philosopher Jacques Derrida.

People who never existed in the Midwest: M*A*S*H's Radar O'Reilly, Ottumwa, Iowa; Star Trek's **Captain James T. Kirk,** Riverside, Iowa; Annie Hall, Chippewa Falls, Wisconsin; Dorothy and Toto, Kansas.

Once upon a time, in the 1870s, visitors to Cardiff, New York, paid a dollar apiece to view a petrified man who was ten feet tall and three feet wide at the shoulders. Scientists pronounced him a petrified man and preachers in turn

Ray Bradbury, Illinois: Fahrenheit 451, Martian Chronicles, *and* The Illustrated Man.

called him "a child of God." He was discovered when excavating well-diggers found him on "Stub" Newell's farm near Cardiff. The truth here was that Stub's brother-in-law, **George, who lived in Iowa,** heard a preacher talking about "giants in the earth" and got an idea. The idea was to have a slab of gypsum cut from a ledge near Fort Dodge, Iowa, have it carved into a human likeness, treat it with sulphuric acid to age it, and ship it to his brother in New York State for the rest of the mischief. Even *after* people learned it was a hoax, they paid a dollar to see it. Make of that what you can.

Soap operas and Chicago have close ties. Irna Phillips invented the first soap in radio, "Painted Dreams." From that auspicious beginning, she developed "Today's Children." Then she was **co-creator of "The Guiding Light,"** and later wrote "These Are My Children." Finally, she developed "As the World Turns." What do you suppose inspired all that? Which fairy tales did she learn as a child? What did she eat for breakfast? What lullabies were sung to her? Irna, talk to us.

Harry Houdini, who was born Ehrich Weiss in Appleton, Wisconsin, adopted the name of Robert-Houdin, **a French magician.** Houdini learned how to flex every muscle in his body and could pick up pins with his eyelashes. He spent time as an acrobat before winning fame for his death-defying tricks. Amazing from the start.

Lake County Museum, in Lake County, Illinois, has 1,500,000 million postcards, if you have the energy to look at that many. Curt Teich, a printer from Chicago, Illinois, who **kept a sample of everything,** is responsible for the collection. Teich was in business form 1898 to 1974. You could write cards to friends until the cows come home.

The Pail and Shovel student political party at the University of Wisconsin at Madison had fun the winter of 1979 by constructing part of the Statue of Liberty—from the top of her crown to the **bridge of her nose** (twenty-two

Anne D. Tallent, South Dakota: Black Hills, the Last Hunting Ground of the Dakotas in 1900.

feet) and from the top of her torch to her wrist (forty feet)—and placing the pieces on the frozen lake for viewers to speculate about. And speculate they did.

Isn't it nice to be wanted? Akeley, Minnesota, is one of how many towns in Minnesota claiming to be home to **Paul Bunyan and Babe,** his blue ox. Brainerd sports a welcoming statue of the big guys at the edge of town. And Bemidji, yet another "home" for the mythic characters, also boasts giant wooden statues. I don't pretend to know what it all means, but I think it has something to do with love.

Folk art has a way of being a comforting pastime for some, but for neighbors, if it's big enough or loud enough or ugly enough, it becomes a nuisance. One Wisconsin success story belongs to Fred Smith, former lumberjack and tavern owner. His delight (not his neighbors') was to create **huge statues of concrete** and paraphernalia next to his tavern. The fish, soldiers, cows, and other subjects captured the attention of John Michael Kohler, bathroom magnate from Sheboygan, Wisconsin, who has discovered and publicized over thirty sites of folk architecture. Under his guidance, the Kohler Foundation purchased Smith's concrete park and donated it to the county in 1973. Perhaps the neighbors have come around.

Nancy Price, Cedar Falls, Iowa: Sleeping with the Enemy. (The movie starred Julia Roberts.)

Living Midwestern

LIVING MIDWESTERN. What does it mean? The weird facts, opinions, quirks, and tales here accumulate to suggest a particular way of living by people of the Midwest—but there's more. These stories and stories like them resonate in Midwesterners because they fit within what might be called the Midwest ethic—the glue that holds the ideas and ideals of the Midwest together. This ethic is not a tidy list of rules that Midwesterners recite each morning but rather it rests in a core deep within us, bubbling up frequently. It is part of what our ancestors brought to this territory, and it has become part of our nature; it affects virtually everything about the way we live. The various ways in which the Midwest ethic expresses itself remains attached to our personalities no matter where we go. For the most part, we bear the attachments proudly, because these laws of life—which might translate into the midwestern "shoulds," even if we don't usually think of them in that way—work for us.

For instance, the fact that we care for each other—are polite and helpful—is useful, besides being satisfying. The fact that most of the Midwest is a relatively safe place is comforting and pleasant. And the fact that we resist taking advantage of each other (sleepless nights, don't you know) is also good; when you can trust the butcher, the baker, and the mortgage-maker, it frees your mind for worthwhile projects, like planning dinner or reviewing the times-tables. The rest of the world may call us a little naïve to carry such trust, but when *everybody's* naïve, it works really well. (This could be why Midwesterners who've moved to one coast or the other have a tendency to hang out with other Midwest-erners. *We know who you are.*)

Somewhere, of course, buried under all of the admonitions about what we as Midwesterners should or shouldn't do lies the original "law of life," the Golden Rule. For some reason, the maxim of doing unto others as you would have them do unto you was a credo that sank deep in the Midwest, and it continues to have a strong influence in daily life as well as in emergencies.

In 1993 the *Orlando Sentinel* published a column by CNN corre-spondent Charles Jaco, in which Jaco described the differences between people's actions during and after the Midwest's floods of 1993 and the Southeast's Hurricane Andrew of 1990. His observations were that neighborly help, vigilance, and a willingness to share available resources marked the flood disaster while the chaos, fear, and damage of the hurri-cane calamity was intensified by looters, hoarding, and price-gouging for essentials.

Jaco ascribed these different responses to the rootedness of Midwesterners versus the transience of the Southerners. There is "an assumption that folks will help one another sandbag, and will not allow one another to be ripped off, because that's just the way people should behave." No one who lived in the Midwest during those floods would disagree.

Living midwestern, of course, "happens" all over the country. By roots or by association, people find themselves dressing more casually. They spend more time walking around their neighborhoods and talking with strangers at restaurants or parks. They begin looking everybody square in the face. These are some of the symptoms.

So some of you readers, I'm sure, are feeling that you may have a bit of Midwest in you, even if you've never ventured farther east than Sacramento (you West Coasters) or farther west than Albany (you East Coasters). Well, it's OK. In fact, it's not only OK, we understand you and we welcome you any time you want to stop by. Five minutes' notice, and the coffee pot's on.

The Midwestern Bill of Rights

We, the people of the Midwest, in order to form a more perfect bond among ourselves as well as to insist on a full place of cultural citizenship among our countrymen and countrywomen, assert our right to exercise our habits, to flaunt our tastes, to indulge in sufficient guilt to get the job done, to gloat over our rising sense of communal self-esteem, to be generally bold in public, and to demand the respect of the rest of the country for ourselves and our children, do present this Bill of Rights to the Nation of the United States and to the World. As Midwesterners, we reserve the right to:

1. Perform actual work when wearing Carhartt coats or Oshkosh bibs.

2. Initiate conversations with strangers in elevators, at gas stations, or wherever the urge strikes us.

3. Eat dinner at twelve noon.

4. Make decisions using only common sense, understanding that horoscopes are there for fun, and to offer a pulse on the mood of the rest of the country.

5. Tune into the weather channel twenty-four hours a day.

6. Consume a meal that is entirely composed of pale food, including but not restricted to: mashed potatoes, apple sauce, boiled fish, rice, pork chops, gravy, scrambled eggs, white bread, and lemon Jell-O or vanilla ice cream for dessert.

7. Mow our own lawns and clean our own houses, even if we can afford to hire someone else to do it.

8. Prepare molded salads with any food item that will fit on either a spoon or a fork.

9. Conduct a meaningful conversation using only shrugs and grunts.

10. Own and drive a car for the purpose of transportation rather than status.

11. Pump gas before we pay for it.

12. Keep personal accounts at our local stores even though we pay with cash.

13. Recognize haute cuisine but nevertheless often prefer low cuisine.

14. Think about cattle when we hear the word "stock" rather than Wall Street.

15. Exercise patience, honesty, and charity in life's dealings, including the most snarled traffic jam, because we know the bottom line is: "Do unto others, as you would have others do unto you."

SOURCES

My Brother, Grant Wood, Nan Wood Graham, State Historical Society of Iowa, Iowa City, 1993; *Handcarts to Zion,* Leroy R. Hafen and Ann W. Hafen, Arthur H. Clark Co., 1960; *Journey to America,* Alexis de Tocqueville, edited by J.P. Mayer, Faber, New York, 1959; *Ethnic America,* Thomas Sowell, Basic Books, New York, 1981; *All Over the Map,* David Jouris, Ten Speed Press, Berkeley, Calif., 1994; *Ask Me Anything About the Presidents,* Louis Phillips, Avon Books, The Hearst Corporation, New York, 1992; *Corn Country,* Homer Croy, p. 216, Duell, Sloan & Pearce, New York, 1947; *Growing Up Indian,* Evelyn Wolfson, Walker and Co., New York, 1986; *Sixty Miles from Contentment—Traveling the Nineteenth-Century American Interior,* M.H. Dunlop, Basic Books, New York, 1995; *The Immigrant Experience,* David M. Reimers, Chelsea House Publishers, New York 1989; *Handbook of Denominations in the United States,* Frank S. Mead, revised by Samuel S. Hill, Abingdon Press by Parthenon Press, Nashville, Tenn., 1985; *Popular Religion in America,* Peter W. Williams, Studies in Religion Series, Prentice-Hall, Englewood, New Jersey, 1980; *Legal Lunacy,* Anne and Tom Condon, Price, Stern, Sloan, Los Angeles, 1992; *Official Guide to Household Spending* 2nd Ed. Margaret Ambry, New Strategist Publications & Consulting, Ithaca, 1993; *The Writer's Guide to Everyday Life in the1800s,* Marc McCutcheon Writer's Digest Books, Cincinnati, Ohio, (p.198 *Chicago Times-Herald* excerpt) (p. 69 Stagecoach Etiquette 1877 *Omaha Herald.*) 1993; *Beer Here,* Stuart A. Kallen, Carol Publishing Group, Seacausus, New Jersey, 1995; *The Wright Brothers, Pioneers of Power Flight,* Carroll V. Glines, Franklin Watts, New York, 1968; *Madonna* Nicole Claro, Chelsea House Publishers, New York, 1994; U.S. Census Data, United States Bureau of the Census, 1990, Washington, D.C.; *Places Rated Almanac,* David Savageau, Prentice Hall Travel, New York, 1993; *Strange Stories, Amazing Facts of America's Past,* Project Editor Jim Dwyer, Reader's Digest Association, Pleasantville, New York, 1989; *A Nation in Motion: Historical American Transportation Sites,* Department of Transportation, Office of Environmental Affairs, Washington, D.C.; *A Pioneer Sampler,* Barbara Greenwood, Ticknor & Fields, New York,1995; *Getting There: Frontier Travel Without Power,* Suzanne Hilton ,Westminster Press, Philadelphia, 1980; *Transportation,* Hazel Jensen, copyright O.J. Fargo, Green Valley Area Education Agency 41, Iowa, 1986; *Churches and Church Membership in the United States,* 1990, Martin B. Bradley, Norman M. Green, Jr., Dale E. Jones, Mac Lynn, Lou Mcneil, Glenmary Research Center /Atlanta, Georgia, 1992; *Iowa Inside Out,* Herb Hake, Iowa State University Press, Ames, Iowa, 1968; *Food from the Heartland,* Glenn Andrews, Prentice Hall Press, New York, 1991; *Kane's Famous First Facts,* Joseph Nathan Kane, H. W. Wilson, New York, 1981; *Susan B. Anthony Slept Here: A Guide to American Women's Landmarks,* Lynn Sherr, Times Books, New York, 1994; *The People's Religion,* George Gallup, Jr. and Jim Castelli, Macmillan Publishing Company, 1989; *Pioneer Women,* JoAnna L. Stratton, Simon and Schuster, New York, 1981; *States Names, Seals, Flags and Symbols*, Benjamin F. Shearer and Barbara S. Shearer, Greenwood Press, Westport, Conn., 1994; *Awesome Almanac— Ohio,* Marjorie Benson, B&B Publishing, Inc., Walworth, Wisconsin, 1995; *Awesome Almanac— Illinois,* Jean F. Blashfield, B&B Publishing, Inc., Walworth, Wisconsin, 1994; *The Midwest and the Nation,* Andrew R.L. Cayton, Indiana University Press, Bloomington,1990; *Cultural Geography of the United States,* Wilbur Zelinsky, Prentice-Hall, Englewood, New Jersey, p.118–119,1973; *American Notes,* Charles Dickens, 1842 report, Fromm, New York, p.168, 1985; *Society in America,* Volume 2, Saunders and Otley, London, p. 327, 1837; Kearney (Nebraska) County History, Volume 1, New York Times Magazine, Mar 10, 1996, *The New York Times,* New York; *Growing up in the Midwest,* edited by Clarence Andrew, Iowa State University Press, Ames, p. 102, 1981; *Early American Winters 1604–1820,* David Ludlum, Boston Meteorological Society, Boston, 1966; *Nebraska Folklore,* Louise Pound, University of Nebraska Press, Lincoln, 1987;

Historical Statistics of the United States—1790–1970, Volume II, The Midwest, University of Alabama Press, Donald B. Dodd and Wynelle S. Dodd, 1976; *Statistical Abstract of the United States 1985–1993,* United States, Department of Commerce, Economics and Statistics Administration, Bureau of the Census, 1995; *Awesome Almanac—Indiana,* Jean F. Blashfield, B&B Publishing, Inc., Walworth, Wisconsin, 1996; *Awesome Almanac—Michigan,* Annette Newcomb, B&B Publishing, Inc., Walworth, Wisconsin, 1993; *Awesome Almana—Wisconsin,* Margie Benson and Nancy Jacobsen, B&B Publishing, Inc., Walworth, Wisconsin, 1993; *The New York Times,* Detroit and Its Octopus Toss, p. 23 April 14, 1996; *History of Green County,* Wisconsin, 1884; *Bound for the Promised Land,* Michael L. Cooper, Lodestar, Dutton, Penguin, New York, 61–62, 32, 59, 66, 72, 1995; *America Eats,* Nelson Algren and David E. Schoonover, The University of Iowa Press, Iowa City, 1992; *Grolier Encyclopedia,* Grolier Electronic Publishing, Inc., 1993; *Shortchanged by History: America's Neglected Innovators,* Vernon Pizer, G.P. Putnam's Sons, New York, 1979; *True Tales of the Old-Time Plains,* David Dary, Crown Publishers, New York, 1979; *From Cape Cod to Dixie and the Tropics,* Report, Negro University Press, New York, 1968; *Domestic Manners of the Americans,* Report. p.36, 1832; Vintage, New York, 1960; *Six Months in America,* Whittaker, Treacher, Volume II, P.279 London,1832; *The Inland Ground, An Evocation of the American Middle West,* Richard Rhodes, University Press of Kansas, Lawrence, 1969; *Sugar Creek: Life on the Illinois Prairie,* John Mack Faragher, p. 237, New Haven Press, New Haven, Connecticut, 1986; *A History of the Middle West, from the Beginning to 1970,* Kenneth Walker, Little Rock, Arkansas, 1972; *Midwest Today,* Midwest Today, Inc. Panora, Iowa, June 1995; *Palimpsest,* State Historical Society of Iowa, Volume 76, No. 1, Spring 1995; *1994 All About Ohio Almanac,* Harry Shay, Editor, Instant Information Company, Hartland, Michigan, 1994; *Indiana, A Bicentennial History,* Howard H. Peckham, W.W. Norton & Company, Inc. New York American Association for State and Local History, Nashville, 1978; *An Excursion Through the United States and Canada, During the Years 1822–23,* William N. Blane, Baldwin, Cradock, and Joy, London, 1824; *Getting There—Frontier Travel Without Power,* Suzanne Hilton, Westminster Press, Philadelphia, 1980; Tour Book: Michigan, Wisconsin, Automobile Association of America, Heathrow, Florida, 1995; *The Best, Worst and Most Unusual Sports,* Stan and Shirley Fifchler, Thomas H. Crowell Co., 1977; *Midwest Living,* Volume 9, Issues 1 ("Hollywood Meets Main Street, USA," Dan Kaercher, p. 6), 2, 3, Volume 10, Issue 4, 5, Meredith Publications, Des Moines, 1995–1996; *The Prairie World,* David Costello, Crowell, New York, 1969; David M. Potter, in his book *People of Plenty: Economic Abundance and the American Character,* University of Chicago Press, Chicago, 1958; *South Dakota,* Dennis B. Fradin, Childrens Press, Chicago, 1995; *Indiana,* Dennis B. Fradin, Childrens Press, Chicago, 1994; *Minnesota,* Dennis B. Fradin, Childrens Press, Chicago, 1995; *Michigan,* Dennis B. Fradin, Childrens Press, Chicago, 1992; *Illinois,* Dennis B. Fradin, Childrens Press, Chicago, 1991; *Iowa,* Dennis B. Fradin, Childrens Press, Chicago, 1993; *North Dakota,* Dennis B. Fradin, Childrens Press, Chicago, 1994; *Ohio,* Dennis B. Fradin, Childrens Press, Chicago, 1993; *Kansas,* Dennis B. Fradin, Childrens Press, Chicago, 1995; *Missouri,* Dennis B. Fradin, Childrens Press, Chicago, 1994; *Nebraska,* Dennis B. Fradin, Childrens Press, Chicago, 1995; *Wisconsin,* Dennis B. Fradin, Childrens Press, Chicago, 1992; Webster's New Biographical Dictionary, Merriam-Webster, Springfield, Mass., 1988; *Gallup Poll Monthly,* The Gallup Poll Organization, Princeton, New Jersey, May, 1994, July 1995; *Great Lives: Nature and the Environment,* Doris Faber and Harold Faber, Charles Scribner's Sons, New York, 1991; *North Dakota,* Robert P. Wilkins and Wynona H. Wilkins, W.W. Norton, New York, 1977; *The World Almanac of the USA,* Allan Carpenter, Carl Provorse, and the Editors of the *World Almanac,* An Imprint of Funk & Wagnalls Corporation, Mahwah, New Jersey, 1993; *If at All Possible, Involve a Cow: The Book of College Pranks* Neil Steinberg, St. Martin's Press, New York, 1992.

ABOUT THE AUTHOR

Carolyn Lieberg was born in Watertown, South Dakota. She has lived in Minnesota, Ohio, and Wisconsin, and spent extensive time visiting friends and relatives in Indiana, Missouri, Illinois, and North Dakota. She has slept in Michigan, Kansas, and Nebraska, but now sleeps, eats, plays, and works in Iowa City where she lives with her husband, her daughter, and her stepson.

Carolyn earned degrees in Linguistics and Non-Fiction Writing from the University of Wisconsin at Madison and the University of Iowa, respectively. She has served as editor of *Iowa Woman,* and as editor of the children's history magazine, *The Goldfinch,* which won the Golden Lamp Award. She was an editor for The Carnegie Foundation for the Advancement of Teaching and is now Associate Director for the Center for Teaching at The University of Iowa.

● ● ●

Wildcat Canyon Press publishes books with a focus on spirituality, personal growth, women's issues, and home and family. Whether books of meditations, short essays, or how-to texts, they are designed to enlighten the hearts and souls of readers.

For a catalog of our publications please write:

WILDCAT CANYON PRESS
2716 Ninth Street
Berkeley, CA 94710
Phone (510) 848-3600
Fax   (510) 848-1326
Email Circulus@aol.com